Bob Feller's
Little Blue Book
of Baseball Wisdom

Bob Feller
with Burton Rocks

Triumph
B O O K S

Library of Congress Cataloging-in-Publication Data

Feller, Bob, 1918–
  Bob Feller's little blue book of baseball wisdom / Bob Feller with Burton Rocks.
    p. cm.
  ISBN 978-1-60078-219-0
  1. Feller, Bob, 1918- 2. Baseball players—United States—Biography.
  3. Baseball players—United States—Anecdotes. I. Rocks, Burton.
  II. Title.
  GV865.F4F45 2009
  796.357092—dc22
  [B]
                                2008054398

This book is available in quantity at special discounts for your group or organization. For further information, contact:

  Triumph Books
  542 South Dearborn Street
  Suite 750
  Chicago, Illinois 60605
  (312) 939-3330
  Fax (312) 663-3557

Printed in USA
ISBN: 978-1-60078-219-0
Design by Patricia Frey

To my wife, Anne
                    —Bob

To my mom and dad
                    —Burton

Contents

Foreword

Most baseball historians regard Bob as the best pitcher of his generation. When a batter came to the plate—and I speak from personal experience—he feared him. He knew that Bob was bringing his best fastball and his devastating curve.

Bob was first in many categories. He was the first pitcher to get paid for gate admissions on days he pitched, something that had not been done before on such a large scale. He changed the way in which organizations viewed pitchers, and it forced Madison Avenue, as well as the commissioner's office, to understand that pitchers could command the same respect as hitters.

When I got to know Bob well over the years, I realized, by the way in which he speaks about his dad, that his father taught him well. The shrewd businessman

that lurked inside of him was the product of good upbringing. I realized that those days of hard work cleaning out barns on the Feller farm really made an impression on him; he valued a hard day's work. He cherished those days spent playing catch with his dad. Legend has it that Bob was playing catch with his father as a kid in the backyard and threw so hard he broke his dad's arm! But that was Bob—he only knew the motto "Full speed ahead."

I think a truer testament to his father's legacy is this book. Bob's philosophy—as seen through his nine tenets, each one representing a different position on the diamond—allows fans to see a side of him that they seldom see: the personal side of Bob Feller.

No truer compliment can be given to his father than celebrating the values his father instilled in him. One of them was fair play. Bob always took African American players barnstorming with him. He was a good friend to Satchel Paige, and the barnstorming tours he organized allowed players who were not being paid well to earn a fantastic day's pay. The money we made for 30 days worth of work was enough to establish our financial security for the off-season. When we played in Wrigley Field in Los Angeles, a minor-league park built by Cubs owner

William Wrigley, Bob packed that place with Hollywood stars and 25,000 fans—for an exhibition game!

Bob was also a trailblazer on the subject of weight lifting. At a time when coaches warned you of the three deadly sins—swimming, playing golf, and weights—Bob carried weights in his suitcases to help build up his arm strength! He never got musclebound, but he always was strong. Even now, at 90, he can still suit up and throw a ball regulation distance. There aren't too many 90-year-olds who can boast that.

Bob speaks about consistency in the book and cites many great players as examples. He should be cited as the ultimate model of pitching consistency. He led the league in wins before World War II, and after missing three prime years of his baseball life to military service, he returned in perfect form to lead the majors in wins after the war. If the Cy Young Award had been around then, he would have had more than anyone to date.

Bob's greatest legacy may well be that, even to this day, he still goes to bat for others who are not enshrined in the Hall of Fame. Fans don't know it, but he resigned from the Committee on Baseball Veterans because the Hall would not elect candidates about whom he was passionate. He lobbies for Cecil Travis, a war hero. He

has lobbied for former Yankees owner Colonel Jacob Ruppert, an irony considering the Yankees were hated rivals of his Indians. He has campaigned on behalf of Lefty O'Doul for his efforts in taking the game to Japan and making baseball truly international.

Bob Feller never shirked his duties, whether in military battle or on the diamond. Always remaining true to the nine tenets in this book, Bob Feller, along with Burton Rocks, treats baseball fans to a wonderful read filled with insight and understanding about a brilliant pitcher and the values that fueled that 104 mile-per-hour fastball!

—Ralph Kiner

Acknowledgments

We wish to thank everyone at Triumph Books and Random House, especially Tom Bast for signing the project and Katy Sprinkel for her vision, foresight, and outstanding editing of the book.

We also wish to thank family, friends, and everyone at Major League Baseball for their support, particularly the entire Cleveland Indians organization.

Finally, a heartfelt thanks to Ralph Kiner for writing the foreword to this book.

Introduction

B ob Feller's Nine Tenets of Success are a testament to his 90 years on this earth and his productivity as a Hall of Fame pitcher.

Born in Iowa in 1918, Bob Feller lived the American dream of playing professional baseball and solidified his place in baseball history as one of the most dominant pitchers of all time with a Hall of Fame career, despite three-plus years of interruption while serving our country to fight for our freedom in World War II. More than just a baseball icon, Bob Feller is a true war hero and has lived his life on and off the field based upon these nine tenets of success taught to him by his parents at an early age. The carefree days of his childhood were spent absorbing both book knowledge and appreciation for a hard day's work.

Just as a team must field nine players on a diamond, and just as the players must play as a team to win and be successful, Feller's mom and dad taught him that he must do his own part if he wants to succeed in life, and that part entails learning and embracing the nine important values learned right there in Iowa on the Feller farm. Whether he was building Oak View with his dad, sharing quality time with his mom, cleaning out the barn by himself, or practicing hoops in the backyard, there was always something being learned and absorbed. Those early days taught Bob how to bear down in the majors, how to stand the test of time and play for the long haul, how to have intestinal fortitude in pressure situations on and off the diamond—and how to live to be 90!

—Burton Rocks

Bob Feller's
First
Tenet for Success

I always say that home isn't just a physical structure. It is a place where parents, if they do their job, teach their kids the values that help them become better men and women.

Family Values

If family values aren't important to a child's development, then I don't know what is. A family is a foundation that gives children stability for the future. In my case, I was lucky to have had the best of families and the greatest of parents.

I grew up in a small town three miles northeast of the larger town of Van Meter, Iowa. We lived in the country on a farm. I look back now and chuckle at how fortunate I was to grow up when I did and where I did. More importantly, I had the most precious gift of all: parents who were not just physically there for me, but present in both mind and spirit. I had a loving mother who supported me unwaveringly and a father who taught me fundamentals about baseball, basketball, and life.

I always say that a home isn't just a physical structure. It is a place where parents, if they do their job, teach their kids the values that help them become better men and women. Pastorally speaking, the Feller farm was quite a sight. We had everything that an idyllic farm ought to have, from grain and corn to cows and chickens. On the farm, I learned values I could not have possibly learned elsewhere.

The country life had its advantages. We knew everybody. There was the druggist, the grocer, and the barber. Going to the pharmacy was one of the best things about going to town. Today, people think of CVS and other big name pharmacies, but back then they were all mom and pop establishments and famous for one thing: milkshakes! The old-fashioned soda fountains in Doris Day and Charlie Chan movies were made famous in the Midwest. *The Andy Griffith Show* and other television shows capitalized on the phenomenon of the Midwest pharmacy. But it was more than just milkshakes, which were always the best reward for a home run or a well-pitched game. These pharmacies fostered in me the importance of community and family. And strawberry sundaes with a cherry underscored the important lesson of enjoying being a kid, of not rushing the clock.

Van Meter had no movie theater. We had outdoor events instead. On Saturday nights we sat in the grandstands and listened to the high school band play. This was the big Saturday night event. During the winter I would tie my flexible flyer sled to the fender of the school bus and slide down the big hill.

* * *

Parents should give kids the greatest gift in the world— their time! Too often, parents give their children money, but no discipline to go along with that responsibility. I'm not criticizing any particular generation because it happens in all generations. There are two types of parents: those that want to be parents and who enjoy it and those who go through the motions and don't put the time in to shape their kids' lives.

A kid's first steps are crucial, whether they be on a baseball diamond or in life. The idea of a parent saying no to a kid is important. While it might not be easy to say no to a child, it is critical to teach him that when no is said, it means *no*, not maybe or yes. It is the nature of children to test the limits of authority—some might say that's their job. But it is the parents' job to discipline and not allow the limits to be bent like handlebars on a bicycle.

5

Coaches should not be babysitters or parents. Kids should know how to behave before they get to their coaches. A lot of younger players today are coming up to the majors in physical shape, but if they aren't in mental shape, they will never be molded. Parents are the only ones who can create formidable, responsible young men and women. Rome wasn't built in a day, and neither do kids grow up in a day. But if the idea of learning responsibility is never taught, then there's a good chance that undisciplined kids will never realize their dreams, in whatever walks of life they pursue.

*   *   *

I've always said that common sense is different than book sense. I think that if a child balances athletics with books he'll come out all right in life. Books teach children facts, figures, and information they need to achieve in academics and in the business marketplace. Sports teach kids teamwork and problem solving—and common sense—that they will incorporate through a lifetime.

I learned how to read and write from my English books; I learned not to show up another teammate (and, by extension, any human being) from playing baseball and basketball. If a fielder makes an error, you don't get

on his case. If you hit a home run, you don't stop, stare, and run around the bases backwards.

Our country's Founding Fathers had book sense *and* common sense. They gave us a Bill of Rights to go along with our Constitution. That Bill of Rights ensures many personal freedoms, but if one's individual freedom adversely affects others one must suffer the consequences. Many times parents omit that part of life when their children observe that their actions have little or no consequences. But on the ballfield, if you show up another teammate, there will be consequences, whether its a clubhouse fight or the loss of a potential friendship. In today's baseball environment, where free agency rules the game, players are acutely aware of this; they know that they could find their opponent today inside the same locker room the next year.

I tell young pitchers today that the most important thing they can do when it comes to public relations and being a member of a team is to think before they open their mouths. I learned that lesson as a young boy growing up in Van Meter; I didn't need the bright lights of a big city to teach it to me. Dad taught it to me underneath the lights of the "field of dreams" we built together.

*   *   *

My mother was a steady, caring influence in my life. Mom always said that she wanted to be there for her children and not just have them, and she honored that pledge. A boy needs to have a mom around, to understand how to give and receive love. She was a registered nurse and a teacher, but she never missed a day to see me off to school and never missed the chance to welcome me home.

I was lucky to have a mother who was such a strong influence in my life. She was book smart and street smart. She was warm and engaging. Her love for my dad, my sister, and me was genuine and constant. She was the rock of our family, the force that held us together.

I played basketball and baseball, and my sister Marguerite's high school loves were basketball and Ping Pong. (I tried to make a baseball player out of her, but couldn't do it.) Marguerite was on the Van Meter High School girls basketball team. She also was the Iowa State Ping-Pong champion, something we were all proud of—dad, me, and mom. Mom was especially proud that Marguerite followed in her footsteps and became a nurse. It was education that she stressed over all else. She was the guiding influence in both of our

lives. She didn't just bring me and my sister into this world, she loved us both and gave us her greatest gift— her time.

I am always glad to see athletes today who publicly pay respect to their mothers. Shaquille O'Neal has commented many times on the positive example his mother set for him. Eagles quarterback Donovan McNabb has a very close relationship with his mom. He even insisted that she star in a series of Campbell's Soup commercials with him. I'm glad to see genuine bonding like that. I wish baseball players would do the same.

It is mothers who can make a young boy believe in himself and give him the tools to become successful. I am living proof of that. My mom always told me I could do whatever I put my mind to, whether it be baseball or science. She told me to pick something I loved and to pursue it with passion. I chose baseball and she was proud of me. I'll never forget the look in her eyes after my no-hitter in Chicago; she was beaming with pride. She made me feel like a little kid once again.

* * *

And so it began in rural Iowa, a childhood dream that took me from our farm to the Big Show in Cleveland.

But the values came from my mother and my father, who taught me the value of a handshake and the importance of a man's word. Gabe Paul brought me back to the Cleveland Indians in 1980 and ever since then I have had a handshake agreement with the organization.

My dad taught me this great lesson—you can lose your health and money, and regain them, but if you lose your integrity, you can never regain it. I knew my dad was right, even when I was 12, but as I went through various stages of life his words rang louder and louder.

He also taught me the value of hard work, and my baseball dreams were borne from that "field of dreams" the two of us built together, side by side.

Bob Feller's
Second
Tenet for Success

Oak View was more than just a ballfield, it was a symbol of hard work, determination, and what can be accomplished if one stays the course. And I learned on that ballfield that if I am truly doing something I love, I am never really working, I am enjoying life.

Hard Work

I got my first taste of hard work when dad and I under-took the project of building me my very own baseball diamond, right in the heart of our own property. The idea of a "field of dreams" was born in Iowa in 1932. My grandfather, Ed Ferret, had a ballfield in his backyard on their farm two miles away. My dad one day got the idea that he could build me a real baseball field, complete with chalk lines, manicured infield and outfield grass, outfield walls, and stands.

He asked me what I thought about the idea and I jumped at the chance. I would have jumped at anything that entailed being with my dad and the family. Building that ball field showed me the power of a father's love for his son. I learned the value of togetherness, the dignity of courage and persistence, and the importance of ingenuity

and "stick-to-it-iveness." It was the greatest gift my dad could have given to me, other than his time and love.

My dad was my first baseball coach, so it was only fitting that he was the architect for this Feller family endeavor. First, dad cut down 20 trees on his own, using nothing but an old handsaw. It took a lot of muscle to fell those trees. We had about 80 acres of timber on our property, most of them oak trees, so we decided it was appropriate to call our field "Oak View."

I often woke up in the morning and looked down from my bedroom window to the oak trees surrounding our little ballpark off in the distance. The field was situated about three-quarters of a mile north of the Raccoon River. In the fall, Oak View shone its best and displayed its beauty for the entire town to see.

The ballpark had everything you could have asked for—and then some. We installed chicken wire, which was 12 feet high. We put in seats for spectators. There were two outhouses—one for the ladies and one for the gentlemen. We charged fans 25¢ per game; doubleheaders were 35¢. The ballpark even had its own soda pop stand!

Dad and I dragged the field and kept it in shape. Building up the pitcher's mound was a part of the

daily routine. We brought in clay and tapped it down, sometimes by hand and sometimes using a team of horses. I'm certain that all of the manual labor I performed to maintain the ballpark made me a complete athlete. Any groundskeeper can tell you that building up a pitcher's mound is no easy task. It's one of the toughest jobs in baseball. It was from that pitcher's mound that I got my first taste of what it was like to face heat, and not just throw it!

Back then every small town had a baseball team. It brought the community together and gave kids a chance to play outdoors in a competitive, yet friendly, environment. Dad managed our town's team and we played at Oak View. All of the young adults in the area played. Dad booked competitions between teams throughout Iowa.

Dad taught me to be a good person, and we played in an era where African American ballplayers were not allowed in the major leagues. We always hired an African American to umpire the games. My dad recruited an African American catcher and pitcher for our team more than 15 years before Roy Campanella debuted for the Dodgers.

Our "field of dreams" became so famous throughout the state that word traveled. Even when I got up to the

big leagues the teams knew of it. Kevin Costner, famed actor and movie director, used our field as the model ballfield for his movie *Field of Dreams*, some 57 years later.

Back then, young teenage guys took girls to a Sunday ballgame. It was just the thing to do. Nowadays, if you asked a girl in a big city to go to a local Sunday game as a date, you'd lose her—she'd jump in a fast convertible for a latte with the next guy so fast it would make your head spin. But back in the day, in rural America, this was the hubbub of activity on a Sunday. We didn't have television, Internet, video games, BlackBerrys, or anything technological. The community was our entertainment.

* * *

Hard work on the farm was the way in which we developed our bodies. Even weight lifting was crude, except for the barbell and dumbbells. There weren't Nautilus machines or gyms. Strong arms came from field work. Cutting down lumber with a crosscut saw worked the shoulders, triceps, biceps, wrists, forearms, and laterals.

Oak View, as we dubbed it, was more than just a ballfield, it was a symbol of hard work, determination, and what can be accomplished if one stays the course.

And I learned on that ballfield that if I truly am doing something I love, I am never really working, I am enjoying life.

*   *   *

Oak View was just one aspect of the Feller farm. We had an old barn on our farm as well, called Feller Farmstead, that was built way back in 1886. The barn still stands today and is in the National Register. The barn represented to me a structure of stability, just like my family. I learned to appreciate its rich history. I think I developed a love of history from early on because of it. I realized that artifacts from the past tell stories, and those stories speak loudly where the voice is now gone, helping me to understand what came before and what might come to pass.

Feller Farmstead was also a shelter from the cold weather that allowed me to play indoors during the winter. Dad and I also played catch in the barn so that I was primed for baseball season when the frost cleared. I firmly believe that constant throwing was the reason why I never had arm problems and why my arm was so strong.

Today's pitchers might take a big workout and then they won't do anything for a week. That hurts the arm.

I did a little bit of throwing almost every day. It was the farm mentality; you can't harvest everything at once. You need to plant, cultivate, and allow time for growth. It takes a little bit every day, whether raising corn or trying to keep a pitching arm loose for the baseball season.

Of course, there was also plenty of work to be done in the barn, too. I shoveled the manure by hand. I fed the horses and the livestock. I baled the hay. I milked the cows, shoveled the grain, and picked the corn. Today, the corn goes to the silos and is shelled. I had to scoop and shovel the cobs into the corn crib.

Outside the barn was a vast and beautiful expanse of crops. Those acres and acres of vastness helped me to imagine that my dreams could be that way, that there were no boundaries as long as I remained true to myself and to what my parents taught me.

The hours spent milking the cows, picking the corn, and throwing the bales of straw and hay around strengthened my forearms, but all that labor also made me a worker, not just a thrower. I was a successful pitcher when I got to the majors because of the farm work. I had the innate sense of how to pace myself, just as I had done with my daily chores on a farm. It's impossible to throw 20 one hundred mile-per-hour pitches in a row,

yet pitchers throw like mad today and wonder why they tire easily. A farmer would never try to toss a hundred bales of hay around and then suddenly milk cows with reckless abandon. All the work gets done, but it gets done in time, as the farmer paces himself. Just like the farmer, a pitcher must pace himself. If he empties the gas tank in the first inning, goodbye pitching arm! If he paces himself by changing speeds, throwing strikes, getting ahead in the count, and slowing the game down, he will be all right for the entire game.

I threw 36 complete games in 1946, the most complete games hurled in a single season since 1916, and four years before Major League Baseball introduced the live ball. I chalked it all up to being able to pace myself. I knew that this ability came from all the farm work I did as a youth.

I was able to thrive, as were my peers, on a four day rotation, because we were well-conditioned. We didn't want our arms to rest too much. We knew that a little bit of work done consistently would make us stronger. It was, as I am proud to say, the farmer's mentality.

When I fed the hogs, pumped the water, and cleaned out the barn, those chores all worked different muscles. Pumping the water meant doing it by using a hand pump

that worked my hands, wrists, forearms, and shoulders like no Nautilus machine could have ever done. My arms, as a result, had long, lean, defined muscles that were made for pitching. My legs were strengthened as a result of cleaning out that barn.

We truly had a full-functioning farm, which meant we even had our own slaughterhouse. We also made our own soap! I learned from my dad what to do and always wanted to help out mother and dad and never had to be asked to do anything. I wanted to do anything I could to help them for all the time they gave to me. I never wanted to be a rebel. I wanted to be a baseball player, a professional baseball player. I know that without my work ethic, I would not have made it into the big leagues—and certainly wouldn't have had the career I had.

* * *

In today's game, hard work starts during spring training. That report date is the real harbinger of spring, portending of the time when players' stats become their legacy. Each player takes the previous season's burdens into spring training, some more than others. Regardless of the player, one thing is for

sure—that spring training is the time when he had better arrive in proper shape. He needs to be physically and mentally sound; his muscles need to be lean and ready for strenuous workouts; and his mind needs to be cleared of clutter and extracurricular thoughts and focused on the upcoming season.

For the better part of spring training, players work to hone their skills and tone up. For the fans, it's a great chance to see their favorite players up close and get their autographs. The teams love spring training because it is an opportunity to hype up the team, sell a lot of tickets and merchandise, and promote team loyalty amongst their fans.

It takes about three weeks for position players to get into proper shape, and it takes longer for a pitcher. If a pitcher has worked out regularly and has thrown in the off-season then he will be fit and in shape by the time a month goes by.

My winter workout regimen included ice skating for cardiovascular and physical conditioning, which worked my legs and my heart. I also played basketball as much as I could for lateral agility, and hunted for hand-eye coordination. I also ran and did a lot of calisthenics. Once spring training rolled around I spent hours practicing

fundamentals, like backing up bases, covering the bag, fielding bunts, fielding come-backers, and throwing to the bases. In the final two weeks of spring training I put the pedal to the metal. I wanted my fastball, slider, curveball, and change-up to be working well, whether or not I got anybody out. It was about perfecting the craft for Opening Day, so when the gates opened I'd be up to the challenge.

Fans want to see strikeouts in spring training, but pitchers need to understand that they must be in shape for the season. They must pace themselves otherwise they'll leave their dead arm in Florida when the team comes north to New York! The whole concept of spring training is to get into game shape, so that when the season starts they are able to help their teams as best they can. Whoever wins the Grapefruit League or Cactus League has no bearing on the pennant come September— unless a star player injures himself, and then there'll be no pennant in September for that team. That's why the outcome of spring training is irrelevant. Some teams that go all out will leave a bit behind when they come north, but the teams that pace themselves have a full tank in April.

Bob Feller's
Third
Tenet for Success

Loyalty is a tough word to ascribe to baseball these days, especially since so many players jump ship for the Almighty Dollar.

Loyalty

Loyalty starts with your team, your boyhood heroes, and your family. More than anyone, Babe Ruth was loyal to the game of baseball. He did so much for the game that it owes him a debt of gratitude.

Fans know the Babe as a part-mythical, part-human presence in the game. I knew the Babe as a bright-eyed kid from Van Meter, Iowa. He was a hero of mine, as he was to millions of other boys like me across the country. Babe was not only larger than life, but also had a reputation for liking children. He loved people and never said no to signing autographs. If you were a kid in the late '20s, you idolized Ruth by instinct. I was no exception to the rule.

Living in Iowa, it was not likely I'd get to Yankee Stadium any time soon, so the next best thing was

watching Ruth up close and in person when he barnstormed across the country with Lou Gehrig. The two of them together were the biggest baseball happening of the day. They toured with their barnstorming teams, the Bustin' Babes and the Larrupin' Lous.

This was my first insight into a phenomenon of that golden era called "barnstorming," a unique tour that these great legends took to parts of the Midwest and South that didn't have major league teams. The proceeds of these exhibition games all benefited worthwhile charities. Babe and Lou even ventured to Japan to play exhibition games. Both genuinely enjoyed interacting with the local folk and playing for charitable causes. They were phenomenal ambassadors of the game of baseball.

As a youngster, seeing the Babe in person made a huge impression on me. I looked at his eyes, his bone structure, his broad shoulders, and big happy face. I saw his hands, large workmen's hands, yet soft enough to cuddle up to a kid.

I can't stress enough that when I was a kid, there weren't iPods or BlackBerrys or ESPN updates. A kid growing up then had only one shot to see his heroes: go

to the ballpark. Every now and then there'd be a photo in the newspapers, but that was rare. New York had the *Daily News* which had great photos, but photos were a rare commodity. Ticker updates back in the late twenties and early thirties ruled the day. A fan's only lifeline to the pulse of the game was the *tick tick tick* of that ticker in the background, while a voice read the results over the radio airwaves to the multitudes who listened at home with bated breath.

Seeing both Lou and Babe on one diamond was something I have not forgotten, even after my Hall of Fame career. Lou had a strong upper body—it was just a gift from God. Even as a youngster I marveled at how strong he was, and Ruth, too. The difference, I noticed, in their approach was that Ruth was a low-ball hitter and Gehrig was a high-ball hitter.

On that memorable day in Des Moines, Babe and Lou were selling their autograph on baseballs for $5, a lot of money back then, but the proceeds went to Mercy Hospital, a worthy cause, where my mother took her nurse's training. I desperately wanted that ball. That $5 didn't come from a father with a fat back pocket, it came from hard work. I worked hard to earn

that baseball. It was a foot race, you could say, to the office.

At the time, a rash of gophers had been destroying the alfalfa and clover crops. Our county had a bounty out on gophers' feet, 10¢ a pair. I hunted, trapped, and caught 50 of them. My dad and I drove the county office with the bushel of 50 and he watched me receive my $5 from the county office. Patting me on the back, he drove me to the ballpark where I purchased the baseball that Babe and Lou signed. When I held that baseball in my hand, it encapsulated the ethos of hard work and dedication that dad had taught me on our farm, and proved that hard work does pay off in getting something you really want in life. I kept that baseball in my room like a trophy, and still have it to this day in my museum in Van Meter.

What fans and critics forget about Ruth is that he was one of the youngest pitchers to ever win a game in the major leagues. He debuted on July 11, 1914 at the age of 19 for the Boston Red Sox. He won more games by the age of 22 than any pitcher in history—except one. He ranks second to me on that list to this day.

Starting in 1915, Babe's first full season in the big leagues, he had three consecutive seasons of 18 wins

or more and two consecutive 20-win seasons—as a southpaw. This was unheard of at the time. Sure, the league had Christy Mathewson and Cy Young, but they were right handed pitchers, not lefties. It was the dead-ball era. Ed Cicotte actually threw the shine ball as a legal pitch. Back then, doctoring the baseball was not outlawed. The Babe also had a disadvantage as a lefty because the batters were mostly right-handed power hitters. The mounds also varied in height from ballpark to ballpark, always favoring the home team's pitcher.

After the 1919 Black Sox Scandal, baseball was in tatters. Ruth single-handedly transformed the game of baseball from the dead-ball era to the home-run era, and he brought integrity back to a game that was riddled with problems. Ruth's trade to the Yankees after the Red Sox's World Series victory in 1918 and his transformation from pitcher to hitter changed the game forever. And in 1921, when Babe Ruth pitched *and* hit for the Yankees, it was truly an unbelievable accomplishment.

Today, there are statistics on everything. The stats help the athletes earn a ton of money and the sports agents love to break the stats, but back then only the

major statistics were recorded. And having a guy like Ruth who threw and hit in the same year was unprecedented. Examining 1921 finds that Ruth went undefeated that season as a pitcher, plus he belted 59 home runs and hit .378, with an incredible .846 slugging percentage in the process! That's what I call special. Ruth did not just hit for a high average on night games in July or some other oddball figure. He had real stats in a real era untainted by steroids.

Babe's number should be retired throughout all of baseball for what he did for the game. The country faith in baseball was dashed after the White Sox scandal, but the Babe's prowess at the plate brought the fans back to the game, so much so that the Giants threw the Yankees out of the Polo Grounds and forced them to get a new home of their own. Babe Ruth was, and is, the greatest player in baseball history. He's the only player who ever pitched and hit at a Hall of Fame level. If he hadn't taken up the lumber, he'd have gone into the Hall of Fame as the greatest left-hander of all time.

* * *

Loyalty is a tough word to ascribe to baseball these days, especially since so many players jump ship for

the Almighty Dollar. But there are still some wonderful players to whom I can point.

Cal Ripken, Jr. played his career in Baltimore and remained true to his Orioles, even after breaking the Iron Man's record for consecutive games played.

Ken Griffey Jr. went to Cincinnati to go home to his family and hometown, and that's more than commendable.

Tony Gwynn never jumped ship from the Padres, and played in just one World Series, in 1998, only to lose to the Yankees. Someone with his career ought to have been in many more, but Tony stayed loyal to San Diego, which I consider admirable.

Mariano Rivera and Derek Jeter have played their entire careers for the Yankees, as has Jorge Posada.

Tommy Lasorda stayed with his Dodgers, having gone from homegrown talent to manager to GM.

John Smoltz has remained loyal to the Braves, as has Bobby Cox as manager and John Schuerholz as GM.

Today players have a lot of temptation to make them jump ship—guaranteed contracts, endorsement opportunities, and speaking engagements. It's easy to say "stay loyal," but harder to avoid the temptation of

holding out in free agency and signing with a big-market team for big bucks.

In our era there was loyalty, but some of it was forced. We hadn't had Curt Flood test the limits of the reserve clause. We didn't have free agency. When Ralph Kiner won all those home run titles in seven years and went to Branch Rickey and asked for a raise, Rickey told him, "We lost with you. We can lose without you." And Kiner never got that raise. Instead, he soon got traded to Chicago and Cleveland.

There was even a rumor that Tom Yawkey and Dan Topping joked about exchanging Joe DiMaggio for Ted Williams. It never happened obviously, but the fact that they thought about it proves that even then owners explored all sorts of possibilities. Ruth wanted to be loyal to Boston. They traded him to New York. He further wanted to remain forever in New York, but they sent him to the the Braves, where he finished his career.

* * *

When the Indians gave me my own statue outside the ballpark I felt that loyalty still existed in sports. The Indians have remained as loyal to me as I have been to them. The statue was unveiled April 1, 1994. The Indians

erected it outside the center-field wall on Ninth Street between Prospect and Carnegie Avenues, in the concourse area of the ballpark. My wife Anne, her daughter Rachel, and my son Steve attended the unveiling and it was nice to share that special moment with them.

At the time I didn't know exactly how I felt about being honored with a statue while I was still alive. It felt strange, and yet I was glad to have the opportunity to see it. The sculptor of that statue was Gary Ross, and he did a phenomenal job on it. It was a really great likeness of me and it was the idea of Indians owner Richard Jacobs, who is a dear friend of mine.

Bob Feller's
Fourth
Tenet for Success

Appreciate the value of a dollar, but also acknowledge that others are entitled to a piece of the pie as well.

Knowing the Value of a Dollar

M y mom and dad taught me the value of a dollar. I didn't get whatever I wanted simply because I asked for it. When I signed my professional contract, I knew that it was hard-earned money that needed to be saved.

I knew the value of a dollar; I came to learn the value of an autograph. Sometimes ballplayers forget that autographs are commodities and that fans are in constant search of them. I feel that signing autographs is a responsibility players should take great pride in—and I tell the stars today that they ought to appreciate their fame and sign them whenever possible.

That having been said, an autograph is a piece of memorabilia, a quantifiable commodity. It can be sold, given away, donated, or withheld. And there is

no guarantee that an autograph will end up in the right hands, either. A player could sign for someone he thinks is a fan but is instead a seller who in turn sells the autograph to a kid for highway robbery. That's something that always irks players, and understandably so. But if the fan is a child, then the player, I feel, has a duty to sign the baseball for him or her.

Most players sign for children and for adults, and most enjoy doing it. There will always be some who won't and who aren't very nice about it, but that's true about doctors, lawyers, accountants, teachers, and anyone in any walk of life doing his job. There will always be good apples and bad apples. The trick in life, I have always found, is to accentuate the positive and avoid the negative. Appreciate the value of a dollar, but also acknowledge that others are entitled to a bit of the pie as well.

* * *

Baseball over the years has become such a big business that organizations have taken the Almighty Dollar as one of their management initiatives, as far as talent goes. Statistics are a great example of this trend. Statistics are great fun for armchair GMs watching the games

on television and playing fantasy baseball with friends. They're great for agents and their clients who reap the rewards from favorable statistics. But baseball has become such a statistically-conscious entity that oftentimes the right players don't reap the right rewards. There are big-game pitchers who hurl 200 innings or more who make less than guys who strike out a lot, but hit 25 home runs. While a player's capacity in the clutch might not be measurable, it is certainly arguable that your reliable pitcher will contribute more to getting your team a win than a slugger. Statistics control the game today because the dollar is tied to them.

My dad taught me that baseball was a business back when we charged fans for use of our Oak View— that part of the game has not changed in 80 years! But baseball needs to do some analysis and find the proper balance. Pitchers who can go deep into games should be rewarded monetarily in accord with hitters who hit home runs (but not at the pace of a Manny Ramirez or a great player like that).

Fantasy baseball is great, but the best baseball GMs are the ones who know the game, not just the stats. A good GM needs to know how a player interacts in the clubhouse. If the guy hit home runs in lopsided victories

but always struck out with the bases loaded, that has to be considered.

Statistics have, and must always be, offset against conditions, no matter what the sport. A great example of how statistics can lie is in basketball: if a court isn't regulation length, then one high school player's stats could be grossly different from another's. Even the NFL altered the game when they brought the hash marks in, helping runners to gain more ground.

Statistics keep people interested and arguing. It's good for the fans so it's good for the game. That said, make no mistake that the numbers have become inflated because conditions have changed. In baseball, the pitcher's mound has been altered. The adjustments have affected how long pitchers can throw, their ERAs, the amount of hits surrendered, and more. Batting numbers have also changed as alterations to the strike zone have been made. The reason I have been vocal about the league needing better umpiring is that the integrity of the game is at stake.

* * *

Baseball today is a bigger business than ever because of television revenue. As I said, years ago it was a business, but the marketing of the game only went so far. Ballplayers

did a few commercials, advertised soaps, and maybe did a cigarette ad or two. If a player was an elite player they got to be on a box of Wheaties. Today, the players have an opportunity to be like partners with the companies they sponsor. David Wright signed a huge endorsement deal with vitaminwater and the stock he received in the company ran into tens of millions of dollars.

This era has allowed for the mass marketing of baseball via satellite providers and cable companies to fans around the globe. Players now retire and go on to create production companies for movies or other big-money ventures. Years ago, when a player hung it up, he sold insurance or did marketing in his hometown. Times have changed since the days of selling door-to-door insurance in the off-season like Willy Loman in *Death of a Salesman*. Players didn't usually do much in the way of marketing while they played.

Lifebuoy Soap was one product that was a marketing avenue for us ballplayers to promote. It was an orange soap and it had a tremendous amount of Lysol in it. It was extremely popular and most players used it; we received it gratis. We smelled like Lysol—even from 20 feet away! Eventually, the manufacturer was able to lessen the odor, much to our delight.

Lifebuoy has a unique little history behind it. The soap was brought over from England where it was originally named the Sunshine Dog Soap. The creator of the soap had developed it for his dog and he decided that if the soap was fit for his English dog, it would be fit for the American public. He did quite well and became very wealthy. Once they extracted that odor from it, I agreed to an endorsement deal with them and it worked out very nicely for me. I even did a commercial with my family for Lifebuoy, which was a thrill.

After retiring as a player I had some interesting sponsorships, including broadcasting the "Mutual Game of the Day," for which I did the 1958 season. For 10 years I endorsed Ivan Combe's family-run company, Combe Incorporated. Ivan was a giant in the personal care business and his products included a number of famous ones like Odor-Eaters, Grecian Formula 16, Lanacane, and Clearasil. He ran product lines for people and dogs. Since his death, his son has run the company; it continues to thrive.

Conrad Hilton's son, Barron Hilton, asked me to become Director of Sports Sales at Hilton Hotels in 1975. I accepted the position and worked there six years.

Once again, my celebrity name allowed me to put a few extra bucks in my pockets.

*   *   *

There was no retirement package for baseball players in my day; we were afforded no compensation and except for the pat on the back, our careers were over without fanfare, media, or monetary compensation of any sort. A player either made it big during his career and could retire or, as was most often the case, had to begin a life of real work in his mid-forties. The problem was that men much younger than him had been working the job market while these men were playing ball, so in the business world, or real world, they had accumulated work experience; all a player had was name recognition.

It was thanks to the determination of Commissioner Happy Chandler—one of the best commissioners the sport of baseball has ever had—and owner Larry MacPhail that the Major League Baseball Pension Plan was created in 1946. The commissioner's office started the players' pension plan with $600,000 in radio rights. It was mutually agreed by players and owners that the players would get 50 percent of both television and radio rights.

Marvin Miller later wrangled a coup in getting the owners to agree to free agency and arbitration—thanks to Curt Flood and Andy Messersmtih testing the waters. Those two individuals were pioneers in the business side of baseball. Catfish Hunter helped break the reserve clause, which was never intended to benefit the players.

Today players have retirement benefits, medical and dental insurance, and a full pension. Players in my day didn't try to make too much hay from marketing themselves. They hoped to make it in the pages of *Newsweek* or *Time*–that was a feat in and of itself. If a ballplayer were truly iconic, *Time* or *Newsweek* would put them on the cover—sports fans were not the audience of these magazines. These were serious periodicals for serious folk. Baseball was considered more of a frolic. A ballplayer hoped to get his picture in the local paper, thereby giving him some attachment and name recognition with fans. This was about the best way a player could get marketed, and if he were marketed well enough then the kids knew his statistics. It was hard for a player to be a celebrity in an era where there weren't many avenues for showcasing the faces of the ballplayers. Technology brought the two coasts together, and made

baseball a national game, instead of a regional game with teams scattered around two halves of the country.

*   *   *

This brings me to the idea of interleague play. Is it good or bad? Was it done for marketing or for baseball purposes? Was it done for the dollar? The answer is yes to the last question.

Interleague play was an idea that was tossed around for years and years before it was implemented in the latter part of the 1990s. It was done for marketing purposes, plain and simple. But has it worked? Has it been good for the game? I think it has. It's given fans in certain baseball cities like Chicago and New York, Los Angeles, and San Francisco bragging rights against their crosstown rivals.

I think interleague play does cut into the natural team rivalries and that certain fan bases would like to see their teams play their traditional rivals more frequently. For instance, the Red Sox fans want to see the Yankees more than they do, and the Yankees would probably like playing teams like the White Sox more than the Mets as far as natural rivalries go, but the hype behind the Mets-Yankees games makes each of their six games almost

like a mini-World Series. It certainly has marketing advantages that are beneficial to some star players. If interleague play continues, I would advocate a four-division league. There should be eastern, western, mid-Atlantic, and midwestern divisions to the splits.

*   *   *

The All-Star Game has also changed. It used to be purely an exhibition game for the fun of the fans and players. Now, the game "counts" since Major League Baseball has decided that the winner of the All-Star Game gets home-field advantage in the World Series. But this was also done for the dollar as well, in an attempt to eke out more drama—and viewership—for the event. But by that decree, if one league keeps winning the All-Star Game, they'll keep hosting the World Series. That, in turn, affects the outcome of the World Series. Years ago the World Series flip-flopped between American and National League host cities on an alternating-year basis. It was fair and equitable. Now, however, the players have more incentive to win the All-Star Game, and the fans are more intent on the game. But the game suffers in that all players don't get in to play if the game is close because the managers are intent on winning.

The idea of the winner of the All-Star Game getting an advantage in the World Series can also affect a team when pitchers might be forced to go more innings than they should. And if they get hurt, the team that they represent will be hurt—and that team might be in the heart of a pennant race. This, in turn, affects statistics for the individual teams and for the individual players involved, both for their All-Star Game numbers and, if they get injured, their regular season stats.

* * *

New ballparks are also a product of modern marketing and have shaped statistics. Ballparks used to be angular, like Sportsman's Park in St. Louis. That ballpark was built on every available inch of real estate in that confined area. Ebbets Field in Brooklyn was a neighborhood park, as was the Polo Grounds. Some time in the 1960s, parks became stadiums. Suddenly, cookie-cutter stadiums were built and dubbed "dual purpose" so that they could be used for both baseball and football. This was good for the teams and bad for the fans. The sight lines were poor. The fans were farther from the action. The ballfields became Astroturf—even the outdoor ones. Veterans Stadium in Philadelphia is one example—the

Astroturf there was multi-colored green as the layers of turf were replaced. It was ugly. Busch Stadium in St. Louis was another circular cookie cutter. Three Rivers in Pittsburgh, Memorial Stadium in Baltimore, and Riverfront Stadium in Cincinnati are all prime examples of circular ballparks that pushed the fans miles away from the action.

Somewhere along the line, baseball rediscovered its history. In the late 1980s, New Comiskey Park in Chicago was made angular like the old one. Camden Yards in Baltimore followed suit. The builders used the natural beauty of Eutaw Street and the old Railroad Yard—Camden Yard—to serve as a natural backdrop to this beautiful new ballpark. Fans were once again close to the action. The sight lines were wonderful. The foul lines were angular. There was not an ocean of foul territory. The seats were spacious and fewer in number. No longer was 60,000 the target attendance, but more like 47,000. Camden Yards was also called a ballpark and not a stadium. It was not designed for multiple purposes, but for baseball only. The Ravens got their own stadium for football right around the corner. Baseball parks were back on the map as real baseball parks.

The Atlanta Braves opened Turner Field, a state-of-the-art, angular facility. The Indians opened a new angular ballpark, as did the Reds, Pirates, Astros, Rangers, Brewers, Cardinals, Padres, and Phillies. All of these ballparks are wonderful because they were designed with the baseball fan in mind. They all share terrific ambiance and offer terrific marketing experiences, including interactive events, wide seats, and big aisles.

The new ballparks have very little foul territory, and they have given infielders limited infield foul territory room for good reason—nobody pays to see a fly ball caught in foul territory. The old ballparks, before the cookie cutter stadiums, had a reasonable amount of foul territory but were still very angular.

If I were a ballpark architect or team owner I'd want my ballpark designed to be 430 feet straight away center field, 350 to 355 feet down the left and right field lines, and 385 to 390 feet down the power alleys. Even with my dimensions, hitters will still send the balls out of the ballpark like homesick angels. The ball is more tightly wound than it was when I played and it's made of cowhide, not horsehide, which makes a big difference. During the home run craze with McGwire and Sosa,

the ball was extremely tightly wound—the tightest ever. The experts have all claimed that the ball was not more tightly wound but I gripped the balls back in 1998, 1999, and 2000 and I *know* that they were more tightly wound for the home run.

Bob Feller's Fifth Tenet for Success

Since I was nine years old all I had ever wanted to do was play baseball. And I knew I could. It may sound cocky, but I was a confident kid with a great arm, a good fastball, and a knee-buckling curve.

Self-Confidence

Since I was nine years old all I had ever wanted to do was play baseball. And I knew I could. It may sound cocky, but I was a confident kid with a great arm, a good fastball, and a knee-buckling curve.

When I was 15 years old, I would go out and pitch for $100 and a tank of gas offered by in-state promoters and managers. My preparedness for the major leagues was borne from my upbringing, and I think that it was one quality that helped me deal with the offers that came my way.

I was playing American Legion ball and McMahon, a bird dog scout for the Indians organization, was the umpire there. He took a good look at me and realized I could play. Suddenly competition between scouts emerged. Ten days later, the Indians' main scout, Cy

Slapnicka was in Des Moines with a contract. The Detroit Tigers approached my dad at the National Amateur Tournament—and even offered him an all-expenses-paid trip to the 1935 World Series at their expense in Detroit! He declined because he didn't want to be obligated to them.

I was 16 and between my sophomore and junior years of high school when I signed my first professional baseball contract with the Cleveland Indians. They gave me $1.00 and an autographed team baseball, which had some great signatures on it including Hal Trosky, Mel Harder, and Earl Averill. My dad, as my legal guardian, signed the contract with me. I still have the canceled check in my museum in Van Meter, Iowa.

I didn't care about the money. What I cared about was having the opportunity to play professional baseball. I didn't care if the Indians had plans to put me in Class D in Fargo, North Dakota, their farm team. All I ever wanted to do was play baseball as a career.

* * *

Growing up on the farm, I ate my Wheaties every day. But while I was pretty precocious as a child and felt that I had a good chance to play professional baseball, never

in my wildest imagination did I think I would be asked to appear on the front of a Wheaties box.

So when Wheaties came calling, I jumped at the opportunity. I signed a $2,500 contract and was thrilled. (I found out later that Shirley Temple signed that same year for $10,000! Then again, I couldn't sing or tap dance and I certainly didn't have pin curls, so I suppose she had the edge in that pitching duel.)

I was astonished to think that kids eating breakfast around the country, whether they were in the big city or on the farm like me, saw my picture. I'd like to think that I gave someone inspiration to reach for their dreams, whatever they were. It is one thing I took seriously in baseball—the idea that kids looked up to me. I never wanted to let anyone down.

As a young boy, I listened to baseball broadcasts that were sponsored by Wheaties. In fact, their ads were read by future president Ronald Reagan, who read the ticker of the Cubs games over WHO radio.

* * *

When I was a kid I loved buying baseball cards because you not only got baseball cards but that smelly piece of chewing gum along with it. I chewed that gum until my

teeth were stuck together and I saved the cards as if they were precious jewels. For me, they were. The players on those cards were my heroes and I wanted to be like them. I dreamed of having my own baseball card one day as a big-league pitcher.

The big-league dream came true for me. I signed a pro contract, and was suddenly a major league starting pitcher, and an All-Star, at that.

Bob Feller's Sixth Tenet for Success

Some call errors lapses in judgment. I call it not knowing the fundamentals of the game.

Practicing the Fundamentals

You can't teach someone how to throw a fastball—or to hit one. There are things that pitchers can do to improve their skill, but innate talent cannot be achieved through instruction. Children naturally show these tendencies at an early age.

The curveball is a different story. Once a pitcher can throw a fastball, he can develop a curve. It can be taught at an early age if the child is willing to do exercises to strengthen joints and muscles in the forearms, wrists, hands, and triceps.

I was eight years old when I learned how to throw a curveball. Yet there is a large public outcry everywhere I go about kids throwing curve balls. Current Indians star Cliff Lee instructed a clinic of children and their parents that kids should not throw a curveball until they are 14 or 15.

People say that it hurts the kids' arms. But what hurts the kids' arms is not the pitch, it's that kids today sit indoors in front of the television or computer and don't get enough natural exercise outside of their little leagues. They don't have strong enough muscles in their wrists and hands, and triceps and forearms to throw the curve.

Cliff knows that most children today don't do those proper exercises, so speaking practically he is right. I believe, however, that if a child is properly instructed on how to exercise the muscles necessary to throw breaking pitches, he can do so without getting hurt.

I tell the young major league pitchers that even if they can throw 100 miles per hour they cannot rely solely on the fastball. Even the great Yankees closer Mariano Rivera throws a cutter in addition to his fastball to keep hitters on their toes.

I have advised many Indians pitchers to keep a book on hitters and record how they fare against them. Pitchers, starting at the high school level, should learn how to understand the game from all facets, and should be able to make notes in a journal about what they've observed from fellow opposing hitters. If a hitter consistently hits the inside pitch, make a note of it and next time throw him a slider low and away, or a fastball

high and outside. With a little observation, a pitcher can make the adjustments to get the hitters out.

I likewise kept a physical book on various hitters in the American League, ranging from Ted Williams to Joe DiMaggio and Phil Rizzuto, from Hank Greenberg and Yogi Berra to not so well-known players. My notes in that journal were integral to my success as a big-league pitcher. Back then there wasn't any instant replay or *Baseball Tonight*. I kept a watchful eye on hitters' tendencies and weaknesses, and dated each entry. This allowed me to chart their progression over time, to see if those weaknesses were exploitable. For example, Ted Williams was a dead low-ball hitter as a rookie, but by his junior year in baseball he fouled off the high fastball and then started hitting it for distance. Ted learned. He learned how to adjust his swing to the high fastball, and modified his timing. The great ones always adjust, the rest do not.

I also made notes on ballparks. Comiskey Park, for instance, played 352' down the line and on average 400' in center. They put in a fence to make it 410', but when the wind was blowing in from Lake Michigan those long towering fly balls that took off like shots from the bat died in the center field swirls.

Fenway Park was a little bandbox where fly balls to right field could hook over the foul pole. They later named that right field pole the Pesky Pole in honor of Red Sox hitter Johnny Pesky, who was known for his craft of being able to hit drives to right field that, by God, hooked around that little pole for home runs.

Shibe Park, where the Philadelphia Athletics played, had its own quirks. The park was fairly small; it was less than 300 feet down the right field line and it played about 310 feet in center. Today it would be called a "hitter's ballpark." Luckily, the Athletics didn't have the pitching to match their hitting—except in 1948 when they were in the pennant race with us that went right down to the wire.

Yankee Stadium was an intriguing place. Its "Death Valley" was in center and left-center field. If Joe DiMaggio had played at Fenway and Ted Williams had played at Yankee Stadium, they would have both set home run records. Yankee Stadium was not only the "House That Ruth Built," it was the house built *for* Ruth, with a short porch in right field. There was something else about Yankee Stadium that astonished me—as a young pitcher,I noticed it firsthand—the tourists packed the place! There were always so many tourists that the crowd was civil. Everyone wanted to see the great ballpark,

for good reason, and ventured from long distances to make the pilgrimage. There was a tremendous amount of history that billowed inside of its cavernous interior corridors. Every kid who entered Yankee Stadium, and every pitcher who took to the mound there for the opposition, realized that Ruth, Gehrig, and DiMaggio all walked inside of those chalk lines, the same chalk lines I walked.

Yankee Stadium was a very fair place to play ball, fair in that the fans were fair folk—I've always maintained it was the fairest crowd in the country. The rest of the parks were filled with "homers." In Brooklyn, the Dodgers fans made up about 100 percent of the attendance at Ebbets Field; in Chicago, Comiskey Park was filled with south side fans of the White Sox; but because Yankee Stadium had so many tourists, it was a fair place for a visiting team to play. If someone made a good catch, he was appreciated.

The Polo Grounds was an interesting park because it played to 255 feet down the line for a cheap home run. Suffice it to say, I didn't enjoy playing there.

*   *   *

We've had a wave of revisionist history in baseball. Nowadays, the older players and writers like to embellish

the old height of the pitcher's mound. That's fine by me, but get everyone should get the facts right. Today, there is a uniform height for the mound. Years ago, that was not the case. The height of the pitcher's mound varied from city to city, depending on the team's star pitcher's tendencies. There weren't any standards regarding degree of slope or its height. The mound in Washington, D.C. was three inches high because Walter Johnson was a sidearm pitcher. For me, the Indians always kept a high mound. I had a high leg kick and that high mound suited me just fine. I had a three-quarter delivery to righties and an overhand delivery to lefties. I was more than happy to have my team adapt the mound to my delivery. Today, it is the pitchers who have to adapt; it evens the playing field quite a bit.

My teammates and I liked the fact that we had to tailor our game to each ballpark. It made the game more challenging, but it rewarded those who could make the proper adjustments to their playing.

*   *   *

Sometimes all the preparation in the world can't account for results. There's the age-old expression that it is better

to be lucky than good. If I had to rank the luckiest things that have ever happened to me, I'd put this experience right up at the top of the list.

It all happened in 1940 on the streets of Chicago.

Lew Fonseca ran the Film Division of Major League Baseball out of the Chicago offices. He approached me after I had pitched a game at Comiskey Park and said that he wanted me to throw against a speeding motorcycle. I accepted the challenge, not knowing what in the world was in store for me.

I was wearing a suit and tie the next morning when Lew picked me up. We rode out to the "test site" at Lincoln Park near Lake Michigan. The police had blocked off the street; it was a big to-do.

Lew had brought along the gloves and balls. He explained his plan and I couldn't believe it. I was going to throw in a race against a motorcycle. Lew showed me the target I had to hit and I couldn't believe it. It was a bulls-eye about the size of a cantaloupe.

I began to warm up and Lew said, "No, stand as if there's a man on first base. This way you'll see the motorcycle take off."

I knew that if I took my full wind-up, even if the motorcycle got ahead of me, I could throw much harder,

so I didn't listen to him. I took my full wind-up instead. The motorcycle got a head start on me, but I gave it all I had and I hit that bull's-eye in dead center and my pitch beat the motorcycle! There wasn't any Hollywood smoke and mirrors. The whole thing happened exactly as it is preserved in the Baseball Hall of Fame. There were two cameramen who did their job perfectly and I hit it on the first try. If I hadn't been that lucky I might still be out there throwing today!

The physicists and mathematicians went to work and clocked the speed of my fastball at 104 miles per hour, the fastest ever measured.

It was calculated as follows: I gained 13 feet on the motorcycle, at 60 feet, 6 inches. The motorcycle was traveling at 86 miles per hour. ($86 / 60.5 = 1.42$; $13 + 60.5 = 73.5$; $73.5 \times 1.42 = 104$)

Later I threw to the full electric zone devices at the Aberdeen Ordinance Plant in Washington, D.C. and was clocked there at 107.9 miles per hour, still the fastest pitch ever measured.

I always believed that Walter Johnson was the fastest pitcher I ever saw. Unfortunately, there were no measuring devices of any kind or any tests performed in his era.

I still get tickled to this day whenever I see the footage of me throwing against that speeding motorcycle shown, whether it be at the Hall of Fame, or at a baseball game. I sometimes show it when I give appearances, along with Abbott and Costello's "Who's On First?"

The motorcycle test was a special experience for me. It is the only evidence of how fast I really was in my youth. It has sentimental value to me, but it also represents the first advances in speed measurements in Major League Baseball. Curiosity as to how fast a pitcher could throw his best fastball abounded since the days when Ruth pitched, which was years before I got to the big leagues. I consider myself fortunate to have been in the hub of it all. I am extremely proud to be the fastest clocked; my 104 mark still stands, as does my 107.9 miles per hour.

*   *   *

My fastball was strengthened by years of farm work and consistent practicing, but my preparation for the big leagues also centered around control.

The fastball is a pitch that is considered "thrilling." All Americans are obsessed with speed, aren't they? But the fastball pitch, however captivating, is a product of

one's natural body. My delivery was a product of old-fashioned farm work. I had built up my upper body from the days on the farm milking cows, picking corn, playing catch with my dad, and playing hoops until I dropped. All those chores force you to use your triceps. The result was that I had built up strong triceps. I was blessed with good bones, good genes, good health, and a natural pitching motion that allowed me to generate a tremendous amount of speed and power.

*   *   *

I also think that my grit and determination prepared me for the day I struck out my age.

Kerry Wood of the Chicago Cubs and I share the distinction as the only two pitchers in major league history that can boast that feat. What I mean is that Kerry Wood, when he first came up to the big leagues with the Cubs at 20 years of age, struck out 20 batters in a single game on May 6, 1998. I did the same when I came up as a youngster with the Indians. I struck out 17 batters when I was 17.

To me, this was the first step in accomplishing my goal, establishing myself as a big-league, big-time pitcher who could go the distance and win for a ball club. I felt

I had something to prove to myself, my family, and the Indians, and I think I proved myself admirably.

I was happy for Kerry when he did the same thing because I empathized with him. As a pitcher who can go the distance in a game, it sends a message to the coaching staff that you are durable and a force to be reckoned with. Other teams take notice and treat you as a strikeout pitcher and a rising star.

That day I struck out 17 batters made me proud and I know that my family was proud as well. I broke the American League record for most strikeouts in a game and tied Dizzy Dean's National League record. It was even more special to me when I struck out 18 in front of the home fans in Cleveland, on October 1, 1938.

It was the last day of the season and I was still only 19 years old! It was the first game of a doubleheader against Detroit and Frank Pytlak was catching. The last batter I struck out was Chet Laabs. It was his fifth strikeout of the day. He swung 14 times, took the last pitch for a called third strike, and boy, was he mad at the umpire! The two of them had a good argument as I celebrated. I had a great curveball working that day.

*   *   *

Batters always want to know what's coming. Sometimes they'll cheat by trying to glimpse what the catcher is putting down and other times they'll try to steal signs from second base. There was even a report that surfaced not too long ago, which former New York Giants catcher Sal Yvars confirmed, that the Giants had used a telescope from center field to look into the clubhouse to steal signs from the Dodgers and other opposing teams in 1951.

The pitcher can minimize this problem by not gripping the ball in the way he is going to throw it until he has his glove over the ball during the windup, where it will be covered. This way, his hand is safely ensconced in the glove and nobody knows what the final grip will be until the ball is way past the hitter for a swing and miss.

If the signs are being stolen from the opposing dugout or from the third base coach's box, the pitcher might want to waste a pitch to see if the third base coach has picked up his signs and is calling his pitches to the hitter. If the batter gets crossed up on the wasted pitch, he becomes a bit circumspect about accepting the third base coach's signs in the future.

As far as the runner on second base stealing signs from the pitcher, the pitcher can help his cause by

creating an indicator sign with his catcher and changing the indicator sign every so often.

As long as a pitcher is watchful, he can prevent the batter from ever knowing what is coming his way.

* * *

Pitchers should throw between starts. They don't do it quite as often today. It's up to the pitcher to set up a throwing regimen, but I believe that some good long distance throwing during spring training and during the season is necessary to strengthen the pitcher's throwing arm.

A great way to strengthen an arm is to pitch batting practice. It was done routinely when I played but you'll never see it done today. Perish the thought that a pitcher throw an extra pitch over the pitch count! The agent will call the manager, the GM, and the owner, and heads will roll!

In Japan, a pitcher starts his warm-up 100 feet from the catcher and comes closer. In the United States, the opposite is true: pitchers warm up about 10 to 15 feet in front of the mound and then make their way back to regulation distance as the warm-up intensifies.

Many managers disagree with the idea of long-distance throwing, let alone allowing their pitchers to

take infield practice, but if I managed today I'd insist on it. I used to throw batting practice in between starts on my middle day of the rotation and I still pitched on three days rest. I did not throw much of a bullpen session before the game, but I did wind sprints.

I believe that after a pitcher is good and loose, he ought to take infield practice. Then, once he is perspiring and properly warmed, he can go all out. Coaches won't agree with me, but I think I'm right.

I use my own life as an example of how it worked out for me. The day before I struck out 18 batters, my roommate and I had a long-distance throwing contest. We threw from home plate into the left field bleachers— 375 feet! Evidently it stretched my arm out pretty well.

*   *   *

Little League is a great way to get kids prepared for baseball, not for the majors, but just for loving the game. It should be used as a recreational technique to prepare the child for early development, and that's it.

The jury is still out on whether it builds up ballplayers. The biggest problem I have with it is the pressure to win. That pressure is not placed on the kids by themselves, but rather by the coaches, parents, and organizers. I say

let the kids play, enjoy the game, make friends, and learn the ideas of teamwork, humility, good sportsmanship, and perseverance. After all, if children associate baseball with parental or coach disappointment or ridicule, then their interest in the sport will be severely diminished. No child wants to be yelled at while playing a game!

Years ago, Dale McMillan, also known as Mr. Mac, created a Little League in Fort Wayne, Indiana and paid expenses so that kids could play baseball. He had one rule that lives on in perpetuity: parents cannot stay to watch the game. They have to drop the kids off and return after the game is finished.

When I coached Little League, I made sure that every kid played at least two innings every game and got to bat at least once.

* * *

I always tell parents that the best way to teach kids baseball techniques is through a trial and error method. I know it sounds commonplace, but it's true. I say it not from the voice of me as the teacher, but rather me as the student.

I learned to play the game with my dad in our backyard. It didn't always go smoothly, but we ironed

things out. I watched the pros play and I emulated them. My dad encouraged me to go with what felt comfortable and to develop it from there.

In my day, it was harder to get a glimpse of my heroes because there was no television and going to the ballparks was not an option growing up in rural Iowa. But I raced home from school every day and when dad got home from work, we played catch. Those backyard catches taught me to develop a motion that just felt natural to me. After a while, the motion became *my* motion and I became a pitcher.

Of course, pitching is different than just throwing. Anyone can just throw the ball, but pitching involves being able to throw the ball hard, with accuracy, and at different speeds.

As a youngster in American Legion ball, I played many infield positions before I became a pitcher and I loved them all.

I just loved the game of baseball. Dad and I had afternoon catches and after dinner catches, but it was all in the idea of enjoying the game, and of having fun with my dad because we were outdoors together doing something I loved. We would even take our baseball gloves and a ball with us to our relatives' homes on

Sundays. We had Sunday dinner and afterward played catch into the evening.

Kids ought to just do what comes naturally to them and not be afraid to experiment when they're young with grips and motions. Soon enough, they will discover what their natural motion is and become pitchers, not just throwers.

I am against specialization at an early age. I believe kids ought to play the positions and enjoy the many facets of the game; it will make them better athletes and teammates if they can experience it all first-hand. They will develop an understanding for what each position must endure and they won't be so shortsighted in the end if an error is made. I see it all the time on television and at the ballpark today—pitchers who throw their arms up in the air if their shortstop commits an error. No one did that back in my day. It would have been called showboating and that criticism of one's defense would not have been tolerated. After all, what about the times the shortstop saved the day with a diving stop to preserve a no-hitter or a shutout? Kids need to understand what goes into each and every position to fully appreciate the game. It is a lesson best learned early.

*   *   *

As a pitcher, no relationship is more important than that between the pitcher and the catcher. Games turn on the interplay of the two and it is important for the pitcher to take responsibility for his pitches. If a pitcher does not feel comfortable throwing what the catcher suggests, then he should shake him off and ask for a different pitch. The worst thing a pitcher can do is throw the pitch the catcher calls for when he doesn't believe in it, and without any conviction. The result will more often than not be a long fly ball over the center field fence for a game-ending home run.

Pitchers and catchers can get on the same page easily by speaking openly with one another about their game plan. They should talk about the hitters, their tendencies, and the out-pitches that the particular pitcher can throw with ease and accuracy. Pitchers should also speak with infielders before the game about hitters' tendencies that they might have observed. Good information comes from good preparation.

I seldom shook off my catcher. If at all, it was maybe two or three times during an entire ballgame—and I usually went all nine. If I did shake my catcher off, I wouldn't shake my head. Rather, I just stood there on

the mound and stared until he put down the sign of the pitch I wanted to throw. I see pitchers nod all the time and shake their heads and it amazes me that they would do this. All it really does is telegraph to the hitter what pitch is coming—or at least allow the hitter to make an educated guess.

The dynamic between pitcher and catcher depends on various factors, one of which is age. For instance, if the pitcher is young and the catcher is a veteran, like Jason Varitek of the Red Sox, then the pitcher will take Jason's advice because he has been around, he is the captain, and he knows the hitters. The young pitcher like Jon Lester will depend vitally on Jason Varitek. On the other hand, if the pitcher is older, like Greg Maddux, and the catcher is younger, like Russell Martin of the Dodgers, then the older pitcher's experience is more relevant. Older pitchers usually want catchers who can pick off base runners and who can drive in runs. Usually, the older pitcher has the last word on any given pitch since, as a veteran, he will shoulder the responsibility of what can and will go wrong with a bad pitch. Some catchers are better pitch callers than others, but it still rests on the pitcher to ensure that that the hitter does not reach base.

*   *   *

Pitching coaches are a new addition to the uniformed men inside the dugout. They are good for the game as long as they don't overcoach. The mark of a good pitching coach is the ability to look over a starting rotation and analyze the throwing motion and mechanics of each of the pitchers in that rotation. A pitching coach must know each pitcher's arm strength and other important variables before handing out instruction that could damage a young talent irrevocably.

Pitching coaches, just like the pitchers themselves, keep books, but their books are on their own staff. The pitching coach wants to know, in a documented record, the number of pitches his man threw and whether he is tiring or not. After all, a pitching coach will not last very long by blowing out his starters' arms or by having them throw what he wants to see rather than what is suited to their delivery style and pitching mechanics.

*   *   *

A lot of guys these days think more muscle means more power. But it won't help you if you are a pitcher because you won't have the flexibility to make a strong release. If you can't bend your elbow because your muscle-bound

arm won't go far enough back to give your ear a tug, you won't have much luck as a strikeout king in the majors either. When a baseball player gets muscle-bound, he gets injured. He needs to use common sense when it comes to weights, no matter what position he plays. Weight training is important in baseball. I've always used weights and have always done physical exercise.

It is an important part of the game of baseball, but must be done responsibly.

Ballplayers should have long, lean muscles, not big fat tree trunks for limbs. That said, a player should not use heavy weights. Dumbbells should be 10, 15, or 25 pounds, no more; barbells or other heavy lifts should not exceed 125 pounds. The medicine ball is a fantastic tool in developing all sorts of muscles used in pitching and hitting, and I like the rowing machine as well. I even used to hit a speed bag, which I felt helped my hand-eye coordination quite a bit. When I was aboard ship during World War II, I did deep-knee bends, chin-ups, push-ups, jump rope, and light weight training, oftentimes twice a day when conditions allowed for it.

This way I got my cardiovascular workout in along with a weight training workout. The delicate balance of cardiovascular exercise with weights is important

because as a pitcher you don't want to be muscle-bound since it diminishes your range of motion. As a hitter you don't want to be too muscle-bound either, as you won't be able to get around on inside pitches.

When it comes to weight training, there is also the law of diminishing returns. After a while you will reach a critical mass and it becomes all about maintaining that fitness. Anything more done to build up more muscle is counterproductive.

I have always believed that the hitters who didn't swing very hard were the toughest to get out because they weren't trying to hit home runs, but just meet the ball. To me, they were dangerous. These were the men who turned possible wins into losses at the speed of light. One such man went by the nickname of "Old Reliable." Mel Allen gave Tommy Henrich that nickname because he kept coming through in the clutch. Henrich never tried to overpower the ball; he just met it with the bat and had a nice easy swing. Stan Spence was another guy who could make you sick to your stomach because he came through in the clutch quite a bit. Nellie Fox, Johnny Pesky, and Bobby Doerr were all tough outs as well—the three are Hall of Famers for good reason. Nellie propelled the White Sox and was a fine defensive

fielder as well. Pesky hooked those home runs around the foul pole at Fenway in right field so well they named the right-field foul pole in his honor, and retired his number. Doerr hit 10 home runs off me, most of them at Fenway Park. Joe DiMaggio was a tough out, too, and hit 10 or 11 home runs off me. Ted Williams, interestingly enough, never hit a home run off me before World War II. After we came back from the service, however, Ted belted about 11 home runs off me.

My approach was to throw the slider to lefties, since I felt that was a good "out" pitch for me. For righties, it was a high, tight fastball—as long as I could throw it hard enough to get it past them.

Sad to say, most teams these days don't focus enough on the fundamentals of the game. For whatever reason, bunting, hitting cutoff men, and throwing to the proper base are not taught, and certainly not drilled in spring training, let alone during the regular season. While the players should know their fundamentals before they reach the majors, many don't. I believe that fundamentals ought to be reviewed once every month by all clubs.

Organizations should invest some time into teaching the kids the fundamentals of the game because games are won and lost, whether managers will admit it or

not, on them. Rizzuto, DiMaggio, Ruth, Gehrig—they all thought the fundamentals were important. Mickey Mantle could beat out bunts—and often did for base hits. Derek Jeter can bunt himself on base. Fundamentals are important, and not just for the Yankees. They are especially important for pitchers.

First, pitchers need to be taught how to back up the bases. They should all be able to snag a cutoff throw and throw to base properly. I see a lot of pitchers grab a cutoff throw and heave it toward first or third base, only to have it sail straight down the right or left field line. Back when I played, pitchers were mandated to take infield practice. They constantly worked on their ability to throw the ball around the infield with ease and security. Even Japan has kept that tradition and still makes pitchers take infield practice and practice the fundamentals of the game. Coaches in Japan teach players to hit the cutoff men with regularity.

Some call errors "lapses in judgment." I call it not knowing the fundamentals of the game. Whatever you term it, it doesn't matter. What matters is the fact that the team lost the game because of a lack of preparation.

There used to be a great game called Pepper. Nowadays teams don't play Pepper in the infield anymore.

Groundskeepers think it disturbs their beautiful landscaping. It may, but it was a valuable tool to teach the fundamentals of the game. Jimmie Reese even had a fungo bat for Pepper games. The sign at Yankee Stadium that read "No Pepper" during the late 1980s was an indication of the changing times, the move away from fundamentals and toward the glitz and glamour of a slugger's game. I'm all for glamour, as long as the fundamentals of the game don't suffer, but there should be at least one player on a team that can bunt with regularity—and hit a bunt that doesn't go straight up in the air and make an easy pop-up for the catcher.

I hear a lot of talk about "small ball." Small ball to me is nothing more than executing the fundamentals in the game properly. Many players today can't bunt. When a manager asks them to lay down a bunt in a critical spot in the game to move a runner from second to third so that they would be in position to score on a sac fly, they have a "deer caught in the headlights" look in their eyes.

So what happened? Unfortunately there is no money in small ball! There is money in home runs. There is money for starting pitchers. There is money for closers. But if a guy lays down a good bunt, he'll probably make the league minimum.

Today, home runs and power numbers rule. While the steroid scandal has tainted recent home run seasons, fans still come to see the long ball. Starting pitchers who are special get paid well, as do elite closers, but good defensive players are less valued when it comes to the bottom line. Drag bunts, hitting behind the runner, stealing bases in tight spots when it counts—these talents have been devalued. Today, stolen bases occur when the score is 7–1 and the runner can pad his statistics with an easy lead. The idea of "defensive indifference" has cut down on running up scores for personal stats, but the logic of "me first" is still prevalent. I don't blame players one bit for trying to make a buck; I would too if I played today. But, I do blame teams for not attempting to teach fundamentals and reinforcing them throughout the season.

The irony of the whole matter is that without perfecting fundamental play, teams are not successful in the end. Rarely does a world champion come from a team that can't hit and run, steal, bunt, throw strikes when it counts, or back up plays when it counts. The teams that emerge victorious in October execute the fundamentals well, or well enough to win. Tony La Russa's Cardinals in 2006 are a great example. The 1998 Yankees played small ball well and executed fundamentals.

My 1948 ball club had a great team and we tried our hardest to play fundamentally sound baseball. We tried, as a pitching staff, to have a nose for where the play was developing. We backed up our bases, hit our cutoff men, and threw strikes when it counted. Larry Doby had speed and stole bases when it counted, when the game was on the line. Satchel Paige was a good fielding pitcher who knew where to be on a given play. Joe Gordon, Kenny Keltner, and Ray Mack were sure-footed infielders who knew how to execute sound defensive plays. We did the little things well, won the big games as a consequence, and became champions.

A good pickoff move has become a relic of the past; it's a throwback to a now-bygone era in baseball when bases were stolen to advance a runner, not a career, and when pitchers knew what they were doing when they tried to hold a runner on. Andy Pettitte has a sensational pickoff move. He manages to get the runner caught in the open, about 15 paces off first base. He's a darn good pitcher and a gamer, competitive and honest to a fault. He's what we used to call a "big-game pitcher."

When I held runners on I stepped off the rubber and stepped back on. I looked in for the signs. I tried to catch a glimpse of the runner's behavior out of the corner of

my eye to see if he tipped his hand and was running on my delivery home. It's the pitcher's job to pitch when the runner is standing still and is flat footed. This is the time the pitcher ought to throw over. If he crosses his left foot over his right to take a step, throw!

BOB FELLER'S
SEVENTH
TENET FOR SUCCESS

Good teams focus, band together, accept marching orders from managers, and do not flinch when the pressure is on and fate lies in the balance.

Leadership and Teamwork

B eing a leader, whether in a military battle or a battle for a tightly-contested ballgame, consists of the
following:

1. The leader needs to be able to organize others
    properly.
2. The leader must deputize, supervise, and take
    responsibility for the consequences.
3. The leader must understand and accept
    accountability before accepting the
    assignment.

Lou Boudreau and Al Rosen were two very good
examples of three qualalities of leadership. They weren't
afraid to supervise, they knew how to deputize, they

accepted the consequences, and most often their decisions were good ones, so their success to failure ratio was good.

These men didn't try to befriend everyone either. They wanted respect, not love letters. They had the intestinal fortitude that a good leader needed when a win or loss was on the line. That's why I've always said that every generation must make its own bad decisions, because history repeats itself and younger generations listen to nobody but themselves. (That is true in every generation, and not a criticism of this youngest generation.) Leadership is often impeded by this lack of reflection, and that is why we, whether as a nation, or as a ballclub, have very few good leaders. Rosen and Boudreau were special. They possessed those executive aspects in their personalities which allowed them to make decisions with which they could be at peace, a quality not often found in many a ballplayer. This doesn't mean that a leader has to be disliked. It simply means that the leader must make decisions that are best for the team, as opposed to what is best for the star player or what will bulk up someone's stat sheet.

Teamwork and leadership go hand in hand. One can't exist without the other. I have seen how good

teamwork can win World Championships and win a World War.

As for the former, my Cleveland Indians banded together and we worked as a team in 1948 to win it all. We fired on all cylinders in pitching, hitting, defense, base running, and managing. We won the pennant outright and won the World Series decisively against the Boston Braves and their infamous duo of Spahn and Sain.

Teamwork and leadership was what built the Feller farm into a fully functioning farm in Iowa, and what I observed as a youngster from my parents on how to raise children and build a loving family. I built that field of dreams with dad and we were a team throughout every step of that process. Teamwork was also what enabled us as a nation, along with our Allied Forces, to win World War II and in the process preserve freedom for the entire hemisphere.

Somewhere along the way baseball has forgotten, that above all else, teamwork is necessary to win championships. A baseball team cannot be just a collection of well-paid players. I write this with the utmost respect for the game and with the hope that every player in the major leagues today wants to be a good teammate above a good player.

*   *   *

I joined the navy three days after Pearl Harbor and I was sworn in on December 10, 1941. I desperately wanted to be a pilot in the air force, but my high-frequency hearing loss prevented me from doing so. I was deeply disappointed. I was quickly sent off to War College in Newport, Rhode Island and then assigned to the battleship USS *Alabama*, which had been commissioned in Hampton Roads. I was given the duty of antiaircraft gun captain on a 40 millimeter quad in the Pacific. First we took convoys to Russia, above the Scandinavian peninsula. There, we sunk the last good ship the Germans had, the battleship *Tirpitz*. From there we went to the Pacific along with the battleship USS *South Dakota*. Aboard that ship I witnessed great leadership first-hand, not to mention great teamwork as well.

*   *   *

The concept of teamwork first crystallized with me when we were sitting in Iceland, at Reykjavik Harbor. A report came over the radio that the Nazis were decorating a German submarine commander for sinking the carrier USS *Ranger*. There was only one small problem with this

report—we were sitting in the harbor right beside that carrier *Ranger*, which was safe and sound.

The incident taught me volumes about human nature. The Germans thought that by announcing victory, the rest of their troops would gain morale and that they would feel as if they were winning the war. The same thing occurred in the Pacific when Tokyo Rose blared propaganda through the airwaves about what they had planned to do to the Third Fleet and Task Force 58. They said they knew where we were. Whether they did or didn't is of issue. What is of issue is the fact that, in the end, their teamwork suffered. Even during recreational hours, the admirals on that carrier taught us teamwork. Whenever we overtook an island, the Seabees (navy construction battalions) would come in and, after all the bombardment, they'd build diamonds on that island for us to play ball. Each island took about a month or two to capture, but when it was all over, we'd have the strength to play ball, thanks to the ingenuity and miraculous work of the Seabees.

* * *

Teamwork is not parents yelling and screaming at their kids when the kids don't excel in Little League—that's just

destructive to the child's social and physical development. Teamwork occurs when a child is encouraged to be friends with his teammates and to come to a teammate's rescue in a tough spot.

Many parents think that they are all miniature forms of Douglas MacArthur, or Admiral Chester Nimitz, or Dwight Eisenhower. These men are icons in military history, but to ask a child to be hypercompetitive at the high school level takes a lot the fun out of the game.

Again, our 1948 Indians club won down the stretch because we all banded together. Steve Gromek pitched well. Satchel Paige was terrific that entire year. Bob Lemon was terrific down the stretch when the chips were on the line. Lou Boudreau and Kenny Keltner guarded the infield like soldiers. We won as a team.

I also can cite my archrival Yankees as a model of good teamwork when they had DiMaggio and Rizzuto—not to mention Red Ruffing. The 1998 Yankees had a solid foundation, a core built around Paul O'Neill, Derek Jeter, Jorge Posada, Andy Pettitte, and Mariano Rivera. Those guys played as a team, they beat up the American League as a team, and they won the World Series in style as a team.

But, true of any good team, at the helm were good leaders. We had Lou Boudreau. The old Yankees had Joe

McCarthy and the contemporary Yankees had Joe Torre. Different generations, but the same result—victory! Why? Because good teams focus, band together, accept marching orders from managers, and do not flinch when the pressure is on and fate lies in the balance.

One player, no matter how talented, cannot single-handedly carry an entire team. He might carry them far, but he won't accomplish anything alone. There is no better example of this than my friend, Manny Ramirez. Manny Ramirez is a sure-fire Hall of Famer—and I don't just say this because we are friends from his Cleveland days, I say this because it's true. When Manny came to the Dodgers, he carried the team on his back for the remainder of the season and got them deep into the playoffs. However, he couldn't get them to the World Series, or even win them the National League pennant. A team needs to hit as a team, pitch as a team, and win as a team to be champions. The Dodgers didn't get it done in the clutch, and even though Manny hit the heart out of the ball and got every crucial hit in every key spot, one man does not a team make. A baseball team needs to be a cohesive unit for it to win a World Series.

The Phillies won the 2008 World Series because they hit as a team, pitched well as a team (or well enough

to win as a team), and each player pulled his weight. Rollins, Howard, and Utley got big hits in key spots. Shane Victorino also came through in the clutch. It was a group effort, inspired by Charlie Manuel, their leader.

With good teamwork comes another key ingredient of winning: confidence. Confidence is the product of preparation, perspiration, anticipation, the will to win, and the ability to deliver. The best teams throughout history have come through with all of these ingredients. Our 1948 Indians definitely had the ability to win. We had Bob Lemon, Steve Gromek, Mel Harder, and Satchel Paige.

Satchel proved that age is just a number and that crafty pitching always beats good hitting. The pennant race that year went down to the wire, down to the last week of the season.

The 1949 Yankees won the pennant in that one-game playoff with Boston. Rizzuto came through, as did Henrich.

The Yankees won in 1978 in Boston, enemy territory, because of good teamwork. True to form, when a team is firing on all fronts, every player comes through in some way. That day in October in Boston, Bucky Dent was the hero.

The 1906 Cubs had Tinker, Evers, and Chance, the double-play tandem that just ate up ground balls. Once again, teamwork led to confidence, which led in turn to wins.

*   *   *

One aspect of serving in our military that carried over into baseball was the never ending theme of planning ahead. It was a necessity during the war and no less necessary on the baseball diamond. While my dad first taught this to me in our backyard, the lesson was reinforced on the USS *Alabama*.

I had always taken my ability to take notes and scout opposing teams seriously, but after I came home from World War II, I tried to impart that idea of preparation to my teammates.

Here is my to-do list of things that a ballplayer needs to do to be a winner.

1. Always be in good mental and physical health.
2. Maintain a good diet.
3. Stay away from alcohol and tobacco.
4. Don't do drugs.
5. Get a good night's sleep.
6. Exercise year-round.

I really believe that this list should be up in every clubhouse across the country, from high school to the big leagues.

* * *

Good sportsmanship means giving credit where credit is due and being a decent human being in the process.

I think professional players should be respectful of fans and act graciously. I understand that baseball has become a form of show business, and that's fine, but there are limits. Without limits the sport would disappear and become a total circus act. I think home runs are great for fans; they want to see home runs. But when the hitter knocks one out of the park and then stands at home plate for the length of an entire aria at the opera house, he is pushing the class envelope to the limits.

No matter how much you have, how far you go, and how high you rise, you will most always run into somebody better! They'll do the job better and work harder. It's analogous to my experience on the All-Star team in Iowa. The first question the player will be asked is whether that player is the best in the conference. If so, is he the best in the state? If so, is he the best in the United States? What about the best in the world? There

are no limits to the comparison. Thus, the solution is to do the personal best that can be done and leave it at that—and be happy with the results.

Good sportsmanship also entails playing by the rules. I hate seeing headhunters out there on the mound. I certainly never threw at anybody. I also feel that if a player is going to be out by 10 feet, but he goes in hard and takes out the second baseman, that's poor sportsmanship. The play is over and that kind of behavior is unnecessary. Sure, a player sliding hard into second to break up a double play is a different scenario altogether. I believe in playing hard, and the latter is a good example of working hard to help the team. The former is a good example of working hard to hurt the team, the team's reputation, and probably to get the team's star player hurt when the opposing team retaliates.

I don't like cheaters—I never did! If a player gambles on baseball it's cheating and he should suffer the consequences. If a player takes performance-enhancing drugs and it is proven conclusively that he did so, then he ought to suffer the consequences too. Rules are laws and are not made to be broken. There must be repercussions. If not, we might as well live by the law of the jungle: the survival of the fittest.

*   *   *

Speaking of leadership, I've known all the commissioners in the history of baseball. I've worked with them all, from Kenesaw Mountain Landis to Bud Selig. If I had to choose the best ones, I'd choose Happy Chandler, Bart Giamatti, Fay Vincent, and Bud Selig.

Happy was a great commissioner because he allowed for barnstorming as well as for players to make back money lost due to service in World War II. He started the pension plan with Larry MacPhail, Dixie Walker, and Johnny Murphy of the Yankees. He tried to get back the players who jumped ship to Mexico for amnesty, and succeeded.

Bart Giamatti died too soon because of heart failure and stress, in part because he took a stand. Pete Rose broke the rules. He bet on baseball and needed to be banished from the game. Bart took that tough stand and stood his ground. He was a true baseball fan. He wore his Red Sox cap on campus at Yale because he was a Sox fan through and through.

As a commissioner, Faye Vincent showed on occasion that his principles were unyielding. He upheld Bart's findings on Rose and continued to be tough, yet fair, in working with the Players' Association and with owners.

Bud Selig has been a good commissioner. During his tenure the sport has changed so rapidly, as has his job. He needs to be tough with owners but not too tough, and tough with players but not overbearing. He has straddled that fine line well. Bud has also maintained that rules are made to be followed, not broken, and if they are broken there must be consequences. Some players are on the ineligible list as a result.

There are a number of managers that have been excellent leaders. For my dad, it was Joe McCarthy, who managed me in the 1939 All-Star Game at Yankee Stadium. Joe fit right into my definition of a good manager. He knew how to delegate authority, he didn't flinch from his duty, and he took control without micromanaging.

Joe Torre is a good manager. He took over the Yankees and created another dynasty team in the mid-1990s to 2000. He managed them to the playoffs every year he was in New York for 13 straight years. He didn't overcoach and he knew how to platoon players, as well as motivate to get the best out of them. He made the team's core players—Bernie Williams, Paul O'Neill, Derek Jeter, Jorge Posada, Andy Pettitte, and Mariano Rivera—believe in themselves. He got the best out of

them and that confidence helped to get the best out of those players around them.

Lou Piniella doesn't get enough credit for being a great manager. He took the 1990 Cincinnati Reds to the World Series and made them World Champions. He took the Mariners of the mid-1990s and made them a contender year in and year out. In 2001, he won 116 games during the regular season as skipper of the Mariners—a league record. I must confess, I think his temper is an act. He is a good baseball man and a showman. Yet there is a layer of sincerity to his act that probably instills the fear of God in his players, which is effective for a manager, since a manager can't be a player's best friend.

Jim Leyland is another great manager. He took the Tigers to the World Series in 2006, won the World Series with Florida in 1997, and took the Pirates to the playoffs for three straight years from 1990 to 1992. Leyland is a good baseball man who knows the game, appreciates the game, and effectively works with pitchers and position players. He also has a good eye for coaches and a skill for delegating authority.

Charlie Manuel is a great manager, and Pat Gillick is a stellar GM, and the one responsible for hiring Charlie. Charlie's a genuine hillbilly and doesn't try to hide it.

He's a simple guy with a simple attitude: win! In press conferences he always sounds like he's chewing the fat with his friends at the local country store, but that's Charlie being himself. He was a good player in Japan and when he came to Cleveland to manage, he helped develop Manny Ramirez into a complete player. His 2008 Philadelphia Phillies are living proof of Charlie's winning ways. He would not hesitate to bench even star players, and he wasn't afraid to pitch young guys like Cole Hammels in pressure spots. Jimmie Rollins, Ryan Howard, Chase Utley, and the rest of the guys rallied around him and won the division. They then beat the Brewers in the NLDS, beat the Dodgers in the NLCS handily, and went on to win the 2008 World Series.

* * *

When it comes to team leaders, one name that is not often mentioned is a former teammate of mine for many years, Hal Trosky. He was a great man and team leader. He compiled a lifetime average of .302 over 11 baseball seasons—and he lost three years to World War II as well! In 1936, he led the American League in RBIs with 162; his batting average that year was .343 and his slugging percentage was a whopping .644. I mention him not

only because he had fantastic numbers that have been overlooked by baseball, but because he was a great defensive first baseman. He was a team leader, a great hitter. He was a big man with a genial personality and he saved my no-hitters for me. Another Iowa farm boy, he lived and died in his beloved state of Iowa. He lived about 20 miles west of Cedar Rapids off Highway 20 and then lived in Cedar Rapids until the end of his life. Hal is a perfect example of a great team leader because he spoke softly when called for, put up the numbers to garner respect, and could dish it out when it counted.

Al Rosen was a good team leader. Sometimes a good leader can lead an army, but not lead a ball club. The two are slightly different because ballplayers do not always conform to authority–they are not compelled to since they are in a sport and not in a war. Al Rosen was both respected by the players for his baseball skill and for the fact that he was a no-nonsense kind of guy who you didn't mess with if he got in your face.

* * *

I've always said that the word *hero* has many definitions, but athletes are not real heroes. I don't believe that the

two words should be used in the same sentence. An athlete should always maintain his or her dignity, but that is the main extent of heroism for an athlete.

To me, the real heroes were the men who fought the Nazis, the ones who didn't return. They were the young men who died fighting for our way of life. In my opinion, heroes do not return from wars; survivors do.

A real hero could be a Nobel Prize winner or a famous physician, a scientist, a policeman, or a fireman—but a hero cannot be an athlete. Athletes seldom put their life on the line. At best, they are role models.

The signers of our Constitution faced death to give us the way of life we enjoy. I wonder if there are many people today who would make that sacrifice. Ballplayers seldom give of themselves to preserve ideals. These men gave up their lives to preserve our ideals.

There is nothing glamorous about war. The lucky ones were like me, who returned in one piece, safe and sound. We were able to resume our lives after the war. I returned to pitch in the major leagues and once again tasted stardom. The real heroes never tasted anything but dust!

What I remember about the World War II years was grappling with my father's battle with brain cancer. Returning from the navy, my father having passed away when I was 24 years old, gave me a unique perspective on life. I realized how lucky all of us living soldiers were to return. I realized that life is fleeting. I realized I was lucky and fortunate enough to get paid to play a game, one that I desperately loved.

* * *

On March 15, 2000 I received an honor that deeply touched me. I am now proud to say that I am an honorary member of the Green Berets, in recognition of my work for our troops in the Vietnam War in 1969. The ceremony was a beautiful one at Fort Bragg in North Carolina and the day took me back in time to my days spent aboard our navy in World War II. It all came back to me, aboard the *Alabama* once again, as if I needed a reminder. I remembered that the lucky ones in that war and in any war were the ones who returned home.

Captain Kirtland delivered a speech to the crew of the USS *Alabama* in late August 1943, a few days after the ship cleared the Panama Canal. The speech was inspiring

and insightful and the excerpt that most intrigued me was as follows:

> *"So it is fairly easy to state a few fundamentals by which these early Americans were able to preserve their lives—in fact these fundamentals were largely responsible for the winning and establishment of our United States. They are:*
>
> *First: Guns and ammunition must be in pink of condition.*
>
> *Second: You must see your enemy first.*
>
> *Third: You must shoot first—there was no second best.*
>
> *Fourth: You must hit first—missed shots might just have well not have been fired."*

To that speech I would add one sentence of my own: "Shoot first, because if you don't, you may not have a second chance."

This is certainly true in life—and in baseball. The teams that have scored first often win. Teams that don't put away their opponents when they have the chance to almost never come back and win. In the 2008 playoffs it rang true when the Dodgers failed to put away the

Phillies when they could have and ended up losing the series in five games. The Mets could not put away opponents down the stretch and lost out on making the playoffs. The 2004 Yankees allowed the Red Sox to come back and win Game 4 of the ALCS, and this allowed Boston to mount a monumental comeback and take the entire series.

We didn't strike first against the Giants in 1954 and they beat us. I've seen recent All-Star Games turn on a blown save or a missed opportunity. Winning is dependent on inspiration, perspiration, anticipation, and execution of fundamentals. Winning also entails being able to see the situation, see the rival team, and striking first to put them away because there are seldom any second chances. The pitchers I like are the ones who can hold a one-run lead through the seventh, eighth and ninth innings.

Bob Feller's Eighth Tenet for Success

*You can't harvest everything at once.
You need to plant, cultivate, and
allow time for growth. It takes
a little bit every day, whether
raising corn or trying to
keep a pitching arm loose
for the baseball season.*

Consistency

When I consider consistency in a team, I can think of none better than the 1948 Indians, of which I am extremely proud to have been a part. In 1948 we played the Boston Braves in the World Series. But that was just the ending to the season, the cherry on the sundae if you will. Our real battle was making it there. We won the pennant by edging out the Red Sox—and it was a nail biter until the end.

I started Game 1 of the World Series at Braves Field in Boston. It was cold and I pitched well, well enough to win, but I didn't get it. Braves catcher Phil Masi was on second base and I picked him off, but the umpire called him safe. He was out, and it wasn't that close a play. I knew I had timed his lead off second base and I got him by about two or three feet. Unfortunately, the umpire

disagreed. The call bothered me then and it still bugs me. Masi ended up scoring on a blooper hit by Braves outfielder Tommy Holmes. We lost the game and Johnny Sain got the win for Boston. Sain was a tough egg. The old expression was "Spahn and Sain and pray for rain," because no National League hitter felt comfortable facing either Warren Spahn or Johnny Sain.

Bob Lemon started Game 2. Bob was a good-hitting pitcher. He began his career—a career that took him to Cooperstown as a pitcher—as a third baseman for Scranton/Wilkes-Barre, the Yankees' Triple-A club. When he returned from the war he was still at third base, though it was during the war that he started pitching and suddenly everyone took note of his great sinker and his good curveball. Lemon also had good control and composure on the mound. He never got flustered. This trait was typical of many of the ballplayers who fought in World War II. You had to have guts to go through what we did; it was not for the faint of heart. Warren Spahn fought at the Battle of the Bulge. He dominated the National League so completely that no lefty had more wins than Spahn by the time he entered Cooperstown in 1973. But Bob outdueled Warren that day at Braves Field and we won the game 4-1.

Gene Bearden won Game 3 for us at home in front of a packed house of 70,306. It was as if we held a football game at Municipal Stadium that day, the crowd was so big. But Game 4 had the Indians faithful fill the house at 81,897, and a record crowd of 86,288 turned out for Game 5. Steve Gromek won Game 4 and I lost Game 5, once again. I didn't have it that day from the start of the game and so we lost.

Baseball is a game of inches. There is luck, there is hitting the ball well, there are the little things that go awry during a game, and there are the frozen ropes that find their way straight into someone's glove.

We came out on top in the end, winning a World Championship for Cleveland, but I was 0-2 in World Series play, even though I had won 25 or more games three times in my career. I led the league in wins for three straight seasons from 1939 to 1941, before being sent off to war, and for two more years in 1946 and 1947 when I returned from duty.

It was a special team in 1948. Pitching with me were Bob Lemon, Satchel Paige, Steve Gromek, and Gene Bearden. We had Kenny Keltner at third base, Bob Kennedy in the outfield, and Larry Doby in center. Doby hit .318 in the World Series for us, and he also had a

good arm. So did Bob Kennedy, his outfield counterpart. The two of them combined for a terrific outfield who routinely made accurate throws. Kennedy had as good an arm as DiMaggio did. DiMaggio was extremely accurate, but Kennedy was better! Shortstop Lou Boudreau hit .273 in the series, better than most of our lineup. Hal Peck, Eddie Robinson, Dale Mitchell, and Thurman Tucker contributed in the cause. Jim Hegan was a stalwart behind the plate in all six games for us. Ray Boone pinch hit for us. Ray, by the way, went on to have some solid years for us and was the first Boone in what has come to be a long line of Boones in Major League Baseball.

* * *

When I think of consistency on an individual level, I think of the great ones, names like Ted Williams, Bill Dickey, Hank Greenberg, Yogi Berra, and Ralph Kiner.

"Teddy Ballgame" was something special. He was what 2000-era fans would call an electric player. He was a game changer. His bat knew no limits. He didn't care about the "Williams shift" that the visiting teams put on him. He just hit over it, or through it—or out of the park altogether. In his prime, he never swung at a

bad pitch! It sounds incredible, but it's true. His eye was just that good. He had a great sense of the strike zone and he didn't give in to pitchers, even in crucial moments.

Ted created strikes. By that I mean that he made the pitcher come in with strikes because he wouldn't give up a corner. Ted would not swing at the "pitcher's pitch"; he forced the pitcher to throw what he wanted to see.

He had quick wrists—probably the quickest I have ever seen. He also had big, strong hands on an athletic frame. He was tall and solid. Some describe him as lanky, but he was a big, strong guy in my book, one who always used his height to an advantage, leaning over the plate and exploding on the ball. People seem to forget that he was 6'4". Ted was no shrinking violet, that's for sure. He was a better low-ball hitter than high-ball hitter, but he knew it and he worked on it. He was constantly in the batting cage working on hitting. He loved hitting. He loved to talk your ear off about hitting.

Ted also was a fantastic fielder and was better at playing left field at Fenway Park than any other left-fielder in the game. His one weakness was his road fielding. He did not play the other parks as well because he wasn't the

fastest runner; he had trouble judging fly balls because of his lack of speed. But that's one small weakness in a sea of reasons why he was the best in that era, or in any era.

He led the league in runs scored three years in a row before World War II, from 1940 to 1942, lost three years to service, and then returned to lead the league in runs scored in 1946 and 1947. He batted .406 in 1941, the last hitter to hit .400 through an entire season, and then hit .342, .343, and .369 respectively, after returning from military service, from 1946 through 1948. He was a six-time batting champion, an All-Star in practically every year of his 19-year career, and carried a lifetime .344 batting average, .634 slugging percentage, and a .483 on-base percentage! He lost years to two different wars—World War II and Korea—and was just as proud about serving our country in battle as he was about belting home runs out of Fenway Park.

If anyone had reason to be bitter about the loss of years, it would have been Ted. In 1941 when he hit .406, he had an unprecedented .553 OBP and a Ruthian .735 SLG. This was not achieved by DiMaggio in his prime or even Mantle. Ted Williams is the only hitter to have hit more than .400, more than .500 OBP, and more than .700 SLG. His eye, as I've said, was unparalleled.

There have been some players who have shown consistency in specific situations, including the following:

- *Hitting with a 3-2 count:* Sammy Hale, of our own Cleveland Indians.
- *Pitching on a 3-2 count:* Jim Kaat. Jim always had good control—and you need control as a pitcher to get out of a 3-2 bind.
- *Hitting on a 3-0 count:* Ted Williams. Ted could hit period. He was the best hitter of all time.
- *Pitching on a 3-0 count:* Me! I had a great curveball and I wasn't afraid to throw it on 3-0. Once, I threw three curves in a row and struck out Lou Gehrig!
- *Shortstop:* Lou Boudreau. I played with him for years and he was the complete package. Phil Rizzuto was also solid defensively.
- *Catcher:* Bill Dickey could do it all—hit for average and for power, he could throw out runners, and block the plate.
- *Center field:* Joe DiMaggio hit for average, power, was sure-footed in the field—and he lost years due to the war.

- *Slugging:* Babe Ruth. Nobody crushed a ball like Ruth. Ruth hit meteors while everyone else hit pebbles.
- *Pure hitting:* Ted Williams was the greatest I've ever faced.
- *Electrifying a crowd:* Babe Ruth was the original showman of baseball. He did it all, from standout pitching performances to home runs to hitting for average. Fans forget Ruth retired with a lifetime .342 batting average.

*　*　*

I think Jimmie Foxx was a consistent home run hitter who gets overlooked as time goes by. Jimmie epitomized home run consistency in his career, stretching from the great 1929 Philadelphia Athletics team until his retirement. He could hit a ball as hard and as far as anyone. He swung so hard that when he connected with the ball, the balls flew off his bat and reached the infield or outfield as if they were missiles rocketed off heavy artillery.

Because his swing was so hard, once the barrel of the bat connected with the ball, it stopped any rotation that might have been on the ball. He did what coaches try

to teach—but to no avail because it's nearly impossible to do with any consistency—to hit the round baseball with the bat square! Jimmie didn't have any uppercut. His swing was perfectly square. He was a good fielder at first, played third base as well, and could catch well, but his greatest attribute was his swing. It was all natural and it was just something that couldn't be taught.

His 58 home runs in a single season are testament to the fact that he could hit for power. His .325 lifetime batting average, lifetime .428 OBP, and lifetime .609 slugging percentage prove that he could do it all offensively. He hit for average and for power, something rarely done in his era or any.

* * *

Mickey Mantle was another consistent player. He personified the small town kid made good. He had a great relationship with his dad. Once, when he wanted to quit the game, frustrated that things weren't going his way, his dad drove all the way to pick up his son, only to let him know that once he quit baseball, quitting in life would get easier and easier. It was a great lesson that he passed on to young Mickey, and a lesson my dad would have agreed with as well.

When Mickey debuted in 1951, Joe DiMaggio was still king in New York as far as Yankee fans were concerned, but it was quickly obvious that Joe's skills were declining and that Mickey was the next young star on the scene.

Mickey not only had a great physique, but he was fast. A switch-hitter with tremendous power, I always thought he was a better left-handed hitter than a right-handed hitter. But he could hit the ball equally as far from both sides. He liked the ball low, and if you gave him a low pitch that he could scoop up, the odds were great that he blasted it for a tape measure home run. He was also a good fielder, and while not quite as good as Willie Mays in the outfield, he had lightning speed on the base paths.

Mickey's true worth was that he was the ultimate clutch hitter. He was the guy you want at the plate and on your side when the game was on the line for all the marbles. Since Mickey was such a great switch hitter—the greatest, in fact—facing him was especially tough.

The best compliment I can pay Mickey as far as his athleticism was concerned, is the fact that even after battling osteomyelitis in his leg, a condition that caused him to limp, he was still as speedy as they came. He was

a great all-around athlete in every sense of the word. He could still get to first in 3.3 seconds. If he hit a Baltimore chop—one of those high hoppers—to an infielder, he would beat it out at first for sure.

Taking over for Joe was no easy task, but Mickey did it. He proved that the torch could be passed from DiMaggio, and in the process won a Triple Crown in 1956. He finished his career with a .298 lifetime batting average, 536 home runs, 2,415 hits, and a .557 lifetime slugging percentage. His lifetime OBP was more than .400 as well, which proves that even by today's standards he was one of the most complete players to play the game as far as hitting was concerned. Ruth, Gehrig, Williams, Foxx, and Hornsby—those were the men before Mickey to have lifetime slugging percentages of more than .500 and lifetime OBP of more than .400.

I pitched to Mickey quite a bit. He didn't hit our staff all that well, but he terrorized the rest of the league. Was he better than Duke Snider or Willie Mays? For me, it's all a matter of opinion. Was he better than DiMaggio? He didn't get as much ink in the papers. He didn't throw as well as Joe did, but he ran the bases better. Could he cover as much ground as Joe? Absolutely.

*   *   *

Ralph Kiner is a true Hall of Fame player, a legendary voice in the broadcast booth for the Mets, and a great after-dinner speaker. However, the best attribute Ralph has is the fact that he is one of the most honest, nicest human beings one could ever meet. I think that is the greatest compliment I can give my friend.

Kiner, like the rest of us World War II generational kids, belted home runs when they counted and he won seven home run crowns in a row, from 1946 to 1952. He was the model of reliability during this period as a home-run hitter.

When Hank Greenberg was traded to Pittsburgh, he took the young Kiner under his wing, and mentored him on many levels from baseball to how to carry himself in high society. Kiner took the advice of Hank, another rare quality in a major leaguer. Most players feel that whatever got them to the big leagues is what will keep them there, and they don't listen to what others have to say—even if it is in their best interest or it comes from a Hall of Famer. But that's human nature; when you are young you don't realize what is in your best interest and you close yourself off to the world.

Kiner was different. He was struggling to hit well and Greenberg gave him some sage advice on hitting when they were in the cage one day. From then on, the two were inseparable and Kiner's career skyrocketed, just like one of his many home runs.

Kiner's lifetime ratio of home runs per at bat was second only to the Babe himself. Barry Bonds has since taken over that spot, but Ralph, in his prime, averaged one home run in every 14 at-bats, which was a feat that would not be matched for some time. I say that because the ratio not only spans the length of a player's career, but also is indicative of his productivity. It's hard to hit a home run once every 14 at-bats. That averages about one home run in every other game or every third game. For a player to do that over an entire career is astonishing.

I played with Ralph in Mexico City. At an altitude of 7,700 feet, Ralph's home runs just shot out of the park. In the thin air of one particular day, Ralph, to my astonishment, hit one 600-foot home run after the next. It was a veritable home run derby in the middle of a ballgame.

Ralph had quick hands, and, coupled with his excellent hand-eye coordination, he was able to turn on

many a pitch and launch moon shots. Ralph was the first athlete to really go Hollywood. He dated Elizabeth Taylor and golfed with Bing Crosby. Crosby even got Ralph into broadcasting, a career which became a Hall of Fame-caliber second career. If Ralph had not been inducted into the Hall of Fame by the BBWAA (Baseball Writers Association of America) as a player he'd have gone in as a broadcaster. He not only holds home-run records, but he holds a record for his syndicated show, *Kiner's Korner*, which ran for more than 40 consecutive years.

In an era where Movietone newsreels ruled the day and photos of ballplayers were a precious few, Ralph earned superstar status. Imagine what he'd have done today with the Internet, FOX, and ESPN!

* * *

Berra may be better known for his "Yogi-isms," but he was the model of consistency on the ballfield, along with his counterpart in the National League, Roy Campanella. Make no mistake about it, Yogi was a great hitter. He won three American League MVP awards—amazing for a catcher, and matched only by archrival Campanella.

He had a tremendous amount of upper body strength and had quick wrists. I always had him pegged in my

hitters book as a wrist hitter. He had the ability to snap his wrists and swing the bat with such torque that the ball usually sailed for a home run or a double off the wall. He was a great bad-ball hitter. I had a better shot of getting him out throwing the ball down the middle than if I tried to paint the corner and put it near his shoelaces.

*   *   *

Stan "the Man" Musial, during the war years and for a good decade afterward was as consistent a hitter as they came. No pitcher wanted to see him approaching the batter's box. I was lucky to be broadcasting the game when Stan recorded his 3,000th hit in 1958—he did it against his archrival Chicago Cubs to boot!

Stan was truly one of the game's greats, and not just by National League standards. He could have done it all in either league. My scouting report on Stan read as follows: *An exceptional hitter with a most unusual batting stance.* He didn't have much of an arm, because he started his career as a pitcher and then hurt his arm, after which he was moved to the outfield, and finally first base. He was a fantastic base runner, a three-time MVP, and a seven-time batting champion, with a lifetime batting average of .331, slugging percentage of .559, and an OBP of .418!

But that's not all—he finished with 475 home runs and 3,630 lifetime hits. Stan plays a mean harmonica, but he played and even meaner bat!

* * *

Satchel Paige was, in my opinion, one of the top five or ten pitchers ever in the history of Major League Baseball. He faced the best, and got out the best. He had a great fastball, a great change-up, and threw from every angle fluidly—and with pinpoint control! This was a man who faced legends like Buck O'Neil and Josh Gibson and got them out!

He did his homework better than anyone else. He knew the tendencies of every hitter in the league, whether a famous hitter or a rookie. He knew how to approach them, what to throw, how to proceed if they got on, and if he sensed a weakness of a hitter he hadn't faced before, he quickly was able to—within the same at-bat—pick up the hitter's flaws and put him away.

Even at the ripe old age of 46 he won 12 games for the St. Louis Browns, proving that when you're good, you're good!

I first met Satchel as a kid in Iowa. I pitched against him when I was 16 years old in Des Moines, and then

again in exhibition games on the West Coast, and during the war when his barnstorming team played against mine. We had a good rivalry and a great friendship.

*   *   *

Phil Rizzuto epitomized the motto, "If at first you don't succeed, try, try, again." When he first tried to break into pro ball, he was turned away at a Dodgers tryout. The man who rebuffed him was Casey Stengel, who didn't believe that he could play. Of course, Casey was wrong. Rizzuto was named American League MVP, a rarity for a shortstop, and he went on to hit more than 200 hits in a single season and became one of the best defensive shortstops of all time. A true Hall of Famer, I always point to Phil as an example of determination and courage.

I always found his broadcasts to be honest and fun. They weren't hokey, they were real. Phil cared about real people and that's why he mentioned birthdays and anniversaries in the middle of a fly ball to left-center. When he died in 2007, baseball lost a great ambassador.

*   *   *

Willie Mays was an electric player. A great base runner and home-run hitter, he *owned* the Polo Grounds during

his playing days. He lost time due to military service in Korea, but he was proud of his service and I have always admired him for that. I have no doubt that he would have broken Ruth's record of 714 home runs if he had not lost time because of the Korean War. His great basket catch of Vic Wertz's long fly ball in 1954 was one of the greatest catches I've ever seen.

Breaking down the numbers is important in Willie's case. He not only finished his career with 660 home runs, but he finished with 2,062 runs scored, 1,903 RBIs and a .302 lifetime batting average. He also had 338 stolen bases. This made him a 300-300 man— unheard of in Mays' era. Mays didn't steal bases just for showmanship; he stole them when it counted, when the game was literally on the line, and he almost always made it.

To this day he remains one of the most popular players of all time.

* * *

Most teams could not pitch to Hank Greenberg without him sending those balls over the fences faster than the pitcher could turn his head. He was a terrifying force with the lumber. A two-time American league

MVP, he was the heart and soul behind the Detroit juggernaut of the 1930s. A lifetime .313 hitter over 13 seasons, Hank crushed them when it counted. He had a .670 slugging percentage in 1940 and had slugging percentages of more than .600 for seven consecutive seasons, beginning in 1934. The Tigers reached the World Series in 1934 and Hank hit more than .300 for the Series.

Greenberg honored his religion and did not play on Yom Kippur; I admired him for that, and I think that the rest of the league did, too.

*   *   *

Joe Jackson was the epitome of consistency before being outlawed from baseball.

I met him in a textile mill in South Carolina—on the second floor to be exact. He was a strong man and a great player. He was completely illiterate; his wife taught him how to sign his name when they married. But I was in awe of him; he was an incredible player. Charlie Comiskey was partly to blame for the Black Sox Scandal of 1919, but Joe did take that money. I have often said Joe should be in the Hall of Fame because of extenuating circumstances and because he had remorse. His case was

different than others who were on the ineligible list, but it's still a tough call.

* * *

There are dozens of players who deserve to be remembered along with their more famous counterparts. One such forgotten legend is a man named Heinie Manush. (His real name was Henry, but that was his nickname.) He played for over 17 years, from 1923 to 1939, for the hapless Senators for five and a half seasons, and led the league in hits in the early 1930s. Here was a guy who when he retired held a lifetime batting average of .330.

Another good, solid player was shortstop Marty Marion, who played for the Cardinals during the 1940s. Nicknamed "the Octopus" for good reason, Marty had a great glove and was a six-time All-Star. The Cardinals won the 1946 World Series thanks to Marion's defense.

Joe Gordon, our Indians second baseman, is another nine-time All-Star who doesn't get the credit nowadays he deserves. Nicknamed "Flash," he was a solid defensive player and I credit him with saving one of my no-hitters.

Mike Garcia won 19 games for us in 1954 and led the league with a 2.64 ERA. He was nicknamed "The Big Bear" and really carried us down the stretch.

Arky Vaughan, who I faced as a pitcher, is another player whose name bears repeating when great hitters are mentioned. He hit .385 in 1935, a record for NL shortstops that still stands today. No one has come close to that mark in either league.

Over the course of his illustrious career, Pie Traynor amassed an awesome 2,288 putouts. His lifetime batting average of .320 is amazing, as is his longevity—17 years in an era during which the baseball was almost always knocking around the infield.

I've selected the men above to illustrate the point that great hitting didn't begin in 2000 or 1969. Great hitting has always been around. Every ball club, not just the big-market clubs, has had great hitters, and we should all take the time to remember these hitters, if only because their records hold secrets that can help hitters today. Guys like Traynor underscore the valuable point that good defense is important. Without good defense, teams don't win championships, and that is true of his Pirates in 1925. They beat the Washington Senators in seven games to win the World Series. Pie Traynor not only had a stellar Series defensively, but he hit .346 over those seven games and drove in 4 RBIs.

The education of every ballplayer should—must— include study of the great history of our game.

As far as pitchers are concerned, every last one of them should make themselves well acquainted with the name Cy Young. It's because of his accomplishments that we have such an award that acknowledges exemplary pitching. Unfortunately, I never won a Cy Young Award (it was not established until 1956, the year I retired). Cy Young won 511 games in his illustrious career, more than anyone before or since. (He lost more than anyone as well.) His lifetime ERA was 2.63—astounding considering the amount of games he played. He also ranks first all-time in complete games, with a staggering 815! There is no way, in this modern era of pitch counts and five-day rotations, that anyone will ever approach 500 wins, much less hang in for 815 complete games.

I knew Cy Young well. He often came around to the ballpark and visited with me in the dugout at the old Municipal Stadium. We talked baseball. I treasure those conversations. Cy pitched in the dead-ball era of the early 1900s, which made him a crafty pitcher.

I feel compelled to comment about the influence of ERA on the Cy Young Award. I have never thought

much of ERA as a baseball statistic. They only thing that matters in my book is whether a pitcher wins or loses. If a pitcher wins 100 more games than he loses over his career, he is a good pitcher.

ERA is an important gauge only when pitchers are in high school, college, and the minors. Once a player gets to the majors, it is up to him to win or lose it on his own. Years ago, when I pitched, we paced ourselves and sometimes allowed extra runs so that we could finish the game for our team and get the win. Today stats rule, for better or worse. Agents worry about their clients' ERAs because it's marketable. If their guy leads the league in ERA, he can get a huge pay raise in the next year—even if he hasn't won that many games.

I'm all for athletes making as much money as they can, but I think that the Cy Young Award has evolved over time. It began as an award for the most wins in a season. I tell people that if votes are taking into account wins *and* ERA, then they must also take into account the team for which the person is pitching—because to be a winning pitcher on a bad club is not as easy as it is on a great club. I firmly believe that all three factors need to be taken into account when handing out the yearly award to the proper recipient.

I've faced off against some big-game pitchers in my day, and I admire a few from today as well.

From my era, I have always thought that Whitey Ford was a big-game pitcher. Sandy Koufax and Don Drysdale were certainly big-game pitchers. So too, was Bob Gibson.

In 1968, Denny McLain won more than 30 games and he is the last to have done so. He had a strong arm, and he kept ahead of hitters. He threw strikes. He had a great sinker. That was his "out pitch," his best pitch. Unfortunately all that Coca-Cola he drank gave him a big stomach, but he was a great low-ball pitcher. In 1968, he propelled the Tigers to one of the most special years in baseball, winning the World Series and helping out a city in turmoil.

From the 2000 era, Mike Mussina is one of my favorites. He has good stuff and has enjoyed a great career. I think the ultimate testament to his durability and intensity is that after so many seasons winning 15 or more games, he threw a 20-win season at the age of 39, becoming the oldest pitcher to do so. Mike has pitched some big games at Fenway for the Yankees and when the chips were on the line, he had the intestinal fortitude to come through in the clutch.

Gregg Maddux is a dart thrower. He hits his spots year in and year out. In his Hall of Fame career he has had a great eye, great hand-eye coordination, has managed to stay healthy, and has had a tremendous record as a fielding pitcher.

* * *

I am extraordinarily proud of my ability to complete games. By the time the 1951 season finished, I led the league in complete games with 22. That accomplishment meant something to me. It meant, win or lose, I finished what I had started. That was a principle that I learned early in life on the Feller farmstead. I attribute my tenacity and dedication to the game of baseball to the influences I got from my dad.

I think I had success because I threw strikes, knew the strike zone, concentrated, had better control that year, and knew my hitters. I may have had personal problems but I kept them under my hat. I wanted to immerse myself in the game and I did that.

* * *

I'm also very proud of my no-hitters. Throwing one no-hitter is a feat in and of itself, and extremely hard

to duplicate. Nolan Ryan threw seven of them, which is incredible! I managed to pitch three and consider myself lucky to have accomplished that. I attribute my success to three ingredients: determination, hard work, and a great defense.

Each and every no-hitter I threw had the basic foundation of a good Broadway play. There was Act One, the suspense when it got into the sixth or seventh inning and I hadn't allowed a hit; Act Two, the thought of despair because, as I got really close, I didn't want to blow any of them; and Act Three was the final act, the elation when it was all over!

My first no-hitter came on Opening Day on April 16 at Comiskey Park in Chicago in 1940. It was a propitious way to begin a baseball season, needless to say. I kept the bats silent on the South Side that day, much to Comiskey's dislike. Just as Chicago is known as the Windy City, it's also known for being bitterly cold on Opening Day, and this one was no exception. At game time the temperature off Lake Michigan was 35 degrees and the wind chill made it seem about zero degrees. It was not a day of American blue skies and spring baseball, but was rather like a good old Norwegian gray day that gave me a helping hand of luck. To top it all off, my mom, dad, and

sister were in the stands that day battling the elements and cheering me on to my no-hitter.

But my troubles mounted in the second. I loaded the bases—a definite no-no if you want to throw a no-no! But, nevertheless, I struck out the final batter to retire the side.

My roommate, Jeff Heath, singled for our cause that day in the fourth, and my catcher, Rollie Helmsley, hit a triple up the alley in right-center field to drive home Jeff.

My nerves were fine, but in the ninth Luke Appling gave me a battle. With two outs, Luke, never one to go down easy, fouled off about eight or 10 pitches. I realized that he was on to me that day so, without even telling Rollie Helmsley, I walked Luke by throwing two pitches well outside. It was an intentional walk in my mind, but since I never told my catcher, it was an unintentional intentional walk, as they'd call it today.

But that brought up Taft Wright. Taft had always been a tough out for me, but my thinking was that I'd rather face Wright with Luke on first with a clean slate than keep throwing to Luke, who was on to my timing.

Taft, however, got good wood on the ball and smashed a vicious liner in between first and second base. Ray Mack, our stellar second baseman, dove for the ball.

He fell on his stomach, got to his feet, pivoted to his left, and threw to Hal Trosky at first. The throw beat the flying Taft by a step, and the game was over.

We won 1–0 and my no-hitter was preserved. Like I always have said, no-hitters are a product of concentration, determination, great defense, and a little bit of luck.

This was the first time in major league history that a no-hitter had been hurled on Opening Day. When I found out about that after the game, I was elated. Here I was a young pitcher and I not only had the distinction of throwing a no-hitter, but I had the equally pleasing distinction of tossing the only Opening Day no-hitter in baseball history. What more could my mom, dad, and sis ask for? I had treated them to something really special.

My second no-hitter was a true homecoming for me as far as baseball went, but it happened on the road and not at home in front of our fans.

The 1946 baseball season was the start of my second life in baseball. I had just come home from serving in the navy in World War II, and we were all anxious to get back to our baseball lives, to a time and place that was not about killing but about beating your opponent. I was proud to

have served my country and wouldn't have traded those years for anything, but I was relieved to be home.

April 30, 1946, at Yankee Stadium will forever live in my mind. The Indians and Yankees were going at it with full force. All the regulars who had gone to war had returned. We had our guys, and they had DiMaggio back. We got off to a good start when Frank Hayes hit a home run off Bill Bevens into the left-center-field bleachers, which quieted the crowd. We led 1–0, and it stayed that way for the rest of the game. But, like I said, the game was not without high drama.

In the bottom of the ninth Snuffy Stirnweiss reached base by way of an infield error with no one out. Tommy Henrich, dubbed "Ole Reliable" by Hall of Fame announcer Mel Allen, was reliable that day and bunted Stirnweiss over to second. I had a man on second in scoring position with only one out! This wasn't exactly where I wanted to be at Yankee Stadium. The Yankees were one of the most dangerous teams when they batted down by one run in the bottom of the ninth. They always seemed to come back and win those games in heroic fashion. And Joe DiMaggio was up!

Joe always gave me a tough at-bat, but I had success against him and kept that in the back of my head. A

pitcher always has a leg up if he can remember that a hitter hasn't fared well against him. I wasn't about to lose confidence in my ability to get Joe out.

DiMaggio was tough that day, but my fastball and curveball were on, and Joe ended up grounding out to Lou Boudreau at shortstop, which sent Stirnweiss over to third. I was only one out away from a no-hitter, but I had a man 90 feet away in the home team's park.

The man who stood between me and destiny was Charlie Keller. He didn't get the nickname "King Kong" Keller because of his nice smile. He got the nickname because of his huge forearms and tremendous strength. Charlie, if he turned on a pitch, could crush it with the best of them.

I knew, however, that Charlie couldn't handle my curve that well, so I started him off with a high fastball out of the strike zone, just to see if he'd bite on it. He swung and missed. I had him behind in the count, 0–1. I then threw him one of my big, easy, curveballs and he choked his bat. The result was a weak grounder to Ray Mack at second, who scooped it up and threw it to Les Fleming at first base to end the game and preserve my second no-hitter.

When Yankee Stadium closed its doors in 2008 I was there for the All-Star Game and took one last look from behind that mound. All the memories of that 1946 no-hitter came back to me as if it were yesterday. Unfortunately, *yesterday* was 62 years prior. Many of the fans in attendance at that All-Star Game weren't born in 1946 when I threw my no-hitter, and certainly none of the players on the 2008 Yankees roster were born in 1946. My solace came in the fact that my Hall of Fame contemporaries were born and remembered my second no-hitter!

My third and final no-hitter came on July 1, 1951. That time I treated our home Indians fans to a date with destiny. Municipal Stadium was packed that day, and it wasn't with Tigers fans. It was one of the largest ballparks, and our crowd went wild. But I still had some drama to get through before crowning the no-hitter. The battle between us and the Tigers always made for good drama, and it represented a battle of the midwestern juggernauts.

Vic Wertz, on my second-to-last pitch in the ninth inning, hit a ball foul by four feet into the upper deck, which made my heart skip a beat. Like I said, baseball is a game of inches. An inch one way, foul; an inch another way, fair—that time I got lucky.

I thought about how to pitch him next, and instinct just took over. I threw the heat and he took a called third strike for the final out! We won the game 2–1. I had a no-hitter because the run that scored was unearned and was a product of the fact that we made two errors in one inning, allowing a runner to reach and to score on errors. Thus, I had given up no earned runs and no hits. What made matters worse was that I was one of the culprits of the errors. I tried to pick off a guy who had reached first base on an error and I threw the ball into center field. It's funny now that I think about it, because I was able to be sloppy defensively and still get rewarded for a no-hitter.

*   *   *

In any argument about consistency in baseball, the role of the umpire need be closely considered. Most sports are games of inches, whether it be tennis, baseball, basketball, or football. In baseball, the strike zone used to be defined. Both the pitcher and hitter knew it, and it was rarely a subject of much controversy. We had some great umpires in my day, men like Bill Klem, Bill Dineen, Jocko Conlan, Cal Hubbard, Bill McGowan, and Red Ormsby. I say they were great

because they were so good at their craft that they were never considered an issue in determining a ball game. A good umpire goes unseen! He is not part of the play, the highlight reel, or anything. A good umpire keeps the strike zone consistent and establishes an order that is never disturbed.

While base umpiring has been, and is, good, umpiring behind the plate has lacked in recent years. It was extremely bad in the late 1990s. I remember watching games on television and in person and scratching my head after some of the calls. The strike zone seemed to be whatever the umpires decided it was on a given day. Sometimes the factors for calling balls and strikes were the time of day, the ballpark they were in, the hitter, who the pitcher...heck, maybe even when their plane was leaving! It reached a point where it became ridiculous and the commissioner's office had to step in to re-establish some control and guidelines over umpires, and most importantly, re-establish consistency in the strike zone.

By and large, the effort has worked. This system has become a check and balance on the umpires. It is good for them and it's good for the game of baseball. There will always be human error, but if the discrepancies are

too great, then the game is tarnished. If the umpires are right far more than wrong when it comes to calling balls and strikes—and if we can see for ourselves that it is so—then the game remains at a high level.

Bob Feller's
Ninth
Tenet for Success

*No one man is bigger
than the game.*

Selflessness

When I think of the word *selflessness* I think of my dad. He was a wonderful man who taught me as much about how to be a good person as he did about how to be a good athlete. He was a caring parent who gave of himself every day.

He loved witticisms and adages, and they peppered our conversations. He was not a big talker; he spoke to the point at all times. He illustrated important examples through "isms" that became part of the Feller vernacular. Yogi Berra may have made a fortune from his wit, but my dad shared with me wisdom that was meaningful and heartfelt.

- Whenever my sister and I would try to convince dad of something that was against his better judgment he would tell us, *"A man*

convinced against his will is of the same opinion still."

- When I acted impetuously or selfishly, he would tell me, *"You can be young only once, but you can be immature forever."* He was right; I've seen that many times in the major leagues and now as an elder statesman of the game.

- My father was not one for running his mouth. He disliked people who spoke incessantly. He used to tell me, *"The less you say the longer it will take someone to find out what little you know."* This is especially applicable to baseball players who sound off to the media without thinking. They get themselves into a hole they can't climb out of and then wonder why in the world everyone is against them. I've seen players take locker room conversations out into the media for public airing and then wonder why their teammates don't want to speak with them ever again.

- My dad was a big fan of history. He believed our history presaged our future. *"The best way*

to judge the future is by studying the past," he would tell me. I've seen this ring true as both a ballplayer and serviceman. As a country, we have gotten ourselves into wars because we did not learn from previous experiences. Some players on the diamond make the same mistakes over and over. How many times have I seen a team that can't bunt a runner over from second to third with nobody out miss out on the playoffs? History would tell the players and coaches to brush up on fundamentals.

- *"Each day is a new day."* It sounds rather commonplace but it's appropriate. Players don't realize that if they treat each day as a clean slate, it is a fresh opportunity. Conversely, if they carry the previous day's luggage into the next day, the same bad results will likely reoccur.

- *"Lost time is never found. Use your time wisely as it is your legacy."* Dad told me this as a young boy so that I would respect the fact that I had a chance in life. I never wasted an opportunity to get closer to reaching my dream.

- *"You can lose your money and your health and regain both. But if you lose your character you'll never regain it."* Dad was right on this one. I've seen people get sick and recover. I've seen guys lose their shirt and recover. Money and health are to some extent out of a man's control. But he has nothing else if he does not control the measure of his character. It is the most important thing in the world to preserve.

- *"Character is your shadow. It follows you everywhere!"* Dad took the previous one a step further and he was right. I always knew that wherever I went in life and whatever I did, what people thought of me would dog me forever, both good and bad. Character can be a halo, a person's best friend, or the label of having bad character can be a person's worst enemy, which is why it is important at all times to behave respectfully and sincerely.

- *"There are no atheists in foxholes."* I guess dad meant that when the chips are down and things are bleak, everyone needs help. Everyone asks God—or someone—for help. Trying to

deny that you do not need assistance is foolish. I agree with dad; no man is an island.

- *"The man who knows how will always have a job working for the man who knows why."* Dad always wanted me to understand how life worked. He taught me not to be cocky about anything. A baseball player is always beholden to the team and its ownership. The players are important but must understand that they are replaceable; no one man is bigger than the game.

*   *   *

There are still some great men, men who have put their team and the sport of baseball ahead of themselves, who should be enshrined in Cooperstown and haven't been. Why not? For starters, many of the Hall's voters don't know the history of the game well enough. But I've seen most of the legends of the game play in my lifetime, from Ruth to Alex Rodriguez, and I know the players who should be in but aren't!

I'm all for regional fans wanting "their" guy in the Hall. Many of them are deserving. Chicago Cubs fans want Ron Santo inducted. Mets fans cry out as to why

Gil Hodges isn't there. Pirates fans have clamored for years about Bill Mazeroski.

They all merit Hall consideration, but Colonel Jacob Ruppert, plain and simple—and I'm no Yankees fan—should be in the Hall of Fame. He is the architect of the greatest dynasty in sports and built that baseball cathedral called Yankee Stadium. He is the man responsible for single-handedly signing Babe Ruth, appointing Ed Barrow as general manager and making the Yankees the renowned sports franchise it was and is to this day! It is criminal that Ruppert is not in the Hall. He has not even been considered. His appointing Ed Barrow changed the face of the Yankees franchise—and with the hiring of Barrow came the hiring of Miller Huggins. Ruth and Gehrig flourished under Huggins, as did Tony Lazzeri and Frankie Crossetti, forming what became Murderer's Row in the late 1920's.

And that's not even accounting for the fact that he snared Babe Ruth away from the Red Sox, which at the time was no easy feat. Ruppert had to first convince the Broadway-loving Red Sox owner Harry Frazee that Ruth should be dealt away by Boston. He started working over Frazee, telling him that Ruth was less valuable to his ball club than the ton of money he would get in exchange from

the Yankees. That money could aid him in his outside endeavors, too. Ruppert knew that Frazee wanted capital to invest in his Broadway show, *No, No, Nanette*. He also knew that he'd be getting in exchange a game-changer, a player who would be the poster child for baseball for years to come. Ruppert knew what he was doing. The fame that Frazee got from the show paled in comparison to the fact that the Yankees became the dominant franchise in baseball. This trade was and will always be the biggest heist in sports history. Added to which, the Babe also was on track for a Hall of Fame pitching career—and as a lefty to boot. If Babe Ruth had stayed in Boston, I know he would have been the greatest left-hander of all time. Thanks to Colonel Ruppert, he went to the Yankees. Ruth's fireworks drew so many people that the Yankees overshadowed the Giants in their own home stadium. They were summarily dismissed from the Polo Grounds, and Ruppert built a new ballpark tailor-made for Ruth, with a short porch in right field to which he could hit home runs.

Lefty O'Doul is another prime candidate for Cooperstown. He played 11 years, beginning with the Yankees, and was a part owner of the San Francisco Seals. He's in the Hall of Fame in Japan, as he tore up that league

when he went over there in 1934. A slender guy standing about 6 feet tall, Lefty hit .349 over an 11-year career in the big leagues and then went on to prove to the world, and to future club owners like Walter O'Malley of the Dodgers and Horace Stoneham of the Giants that baseball could, and should, flourish in California.

Pete Browning should be in the Hall of Fame, too, but he has never been put forth to the Baseball Writers Association of America. Most of the writers are too young to have even heard of him, but he deserves it. He had a lifetime average of .341 and an OBP of .403! He led the league in hitting three times with batting averages of .378, .362, and .373. He played for the St. Louis Browns in 1882 where his rookie average at age 21 was .378. He also led the American League in hitting that year. If that doesn't merit the Hall of Fame, having a lifetime batting average of .341 over a 13-year career should.

Cecil Travis also deserves a plaque. He hit .359 in 1941 and held a career lifetime average of .314 over 12 seasons. His career was shortened because of World War II service. During World War II, he froze his feet off at the Battle of the Bulge and never got feeling back to his feet. His injury ended his baseball career at the age of

only 34. He should be in the Hall of Fame both for his career and for his service to our country. The Hall should do the right thing in electing him.

Lastly, I feel Buck O'Neil should be in the Hall of Fame. He was an All-Star player in the Negro Leagues, a tremendous ambassador to the game of baseball, and was instrumental in helping fellow players get elected to Cooperstown. As a player, he swung a great bat, played the infield well, was fast, and was a great defensive player for the Kansas City Monarchs.

* * *

If I had to conjure one last selfless act of grace in baseball, it would be this one.

Babe Ruth's farewell address at Yankee Stadium came against our Indians. It was not a day for rooting. It was a day of appreciation. Everyone in our Indians locker room appreciated the Babe, and what he meant to the game. He *was* baseball. He defined the game for millions of kids, and for millions more yet unborn.

But on that day, June 13, 1948 Babe used my bat to prop himself up—and it wasn't by choice, though I'd have liked it if it was.

Babe was terminally ill, and knew his dire fate.

I couldn't believe that the man who was once called the "Sultan of Swat" now seemed so feeble. He was a rock upon which baseball, and Commissioner Landis, leaned for strength after the 1919 White Sox scandal. He brought the integrity back to the game it so desperately needed.

I saw the Babe play as a kid. I idolized him. I admired what he stood for. Now, seeing the Babe, the Sultan of Swat, battle cancer was a tough pill to swallow. We all get old, and a lot of times not gracefully, if we're lucky even to get there. But Babe got old young. He died young. He left us all way too young.

He staggered inside the tunnel, making it into the dugout. He then took about three steps, approached the bat rack, and selected from three bats. The bat he selected was used as a crutch to lean against as he walked to home plate. That bat was my bat. I felt honored, even if it was just coincidence, that he was using *my* bat. After the ceremony was over he walked back to the dugout using the bat, and put it back in the rack. Then he paused and signed it, returning it once again to the rack. I was elated.

(But the story concerning my bat doesn't end there. I treasured that bat, and yet one of my very own teammates

stole that bat from me. It wasn't accidental; it was stolen. I never saw it again until famed memorabilia collector Barry Halper put it on the market. I bought it back later for $95,000.)When I saw Derek Jeter and Mariano Rivera close Yankee Stadium, and watched Mike Mussina gather dirt from the pitcher's mound and pile it into a cup, it hit home that the stadium in which I had spent a good portion of my youth, both as a pitcher and imagining it as a kid in Iowa idolizing Babe Ruth, was suddenly no more. An era had ended. But, akin to my dad's aphorism, the sorrow vanished the next day and the sun shone on the new ballpark, the new façade, and a new beginning.

The secret of Babe is that he still lives inside of us, and the secret of life is taking the memories of the past and building with them a new future. Babe never lived in the past. He lived in the present. He enjoyed every day of his life. I hope the young guys on the Yankees—and in the rest of the league—do the same.

Afterword

Leaving home was difficult for me. I was young, impressionable, and had lived on a farm for my entire childhood. To be thrust at 17 into the wide world and to be on my own with a big-league ballclub was an extreme culture shock for me. Gradually, Cleveland became a new home. I got to know the locals. I got to know the neighborhoods and where I wanted to live.

In the summer of 1948 I made Gates Mills, Ohio my permanent home. The year we won the World Series seemed like a good enough time for it. I had turned 30 and was a young man on my own. Since that time I've loved the past decades there, over half a century.

When I came back home to Iowa, it was bittersweet. Dad had died. I had lost four of my best baseball years overseas while the game had gone on without me. I felt

a big void in my life. The fans welcomed all of us home with open arms—unlike after some wars—and we were treated as heroes. Being treated as a hero, as I said before, made me feel uneasy because I felt that the real heroes were the men who didn't come back alive.

I felt proud to have served our country, to have made my mom and dad proud by serving, but relieved to be home. The postwar period in baseball and in American history was a time of renaissance in our culture. Before it, we still were a rather innocent nation and we still had our values, both on and off the field.

The sport of baseball has been wonderful to me. It has afforded me the opportunity to live out my childhood dreams, to go from the cornfields of Iowa to the small towns to the big cities around the country, and to many countries around the world. I've also sat down with and have been humbled by players like Ruth, Cobb, Irvin, O'Neil, Paige, DiMaggio, Gehrig, and Dickey.

I still enjoy the induction weekends at Cooperstown. I still enjoy spring training, and suiting up in uniform.

I created my own museum to share these experiences with others. The Bob Feller Museum in Van Meter, Iowa, has allowed visitors from all over the country to come and see some great baseball artifacts and learn some history

about the game and about me. My wife, Anne, a lighting specialist, designed the lighting. The museum has any personal belongings including candy bar wrappers, rare photographs, bats, caps, uniforms, and other interesting artifacts.

My baseball family is extraordinarily important to me, but my own is even more precious. I have three wonderful sons: Steve, Marty, and Bruce. I've had a wonderful marriage to Anne, who has a daughter, Rachel, and a son, John.

I enjoy hanging out with my grandson, Daniel, and watching his pitching career as it flourishes.

I like talking to the people, to the fans, to the ushers, to the new crop of ballplayers. I like being a mentor, and I hope that the younger generation will heed my words as wisdom from someone who's been around.

My current home is out in the woods, and it has particularly special meaning because it was designed by my son Steve. My wife Anne and I reside there, along with our little pal Felix. Felix is our black cat and he follows me everywhere. We have a couple of barns, a gazebo, decks, and a patio. We have our own well water, power, and a full generator in case of an emergency. I feel lucky because I have a taste of what I had as a kid by living

in the country, and I'm just 22 miles away from Jacobs Field in downtown Cleveland. I can visit any night and walk into the clubhouse whenever I want.

* * *

Someone once wrote a book on living to 100. He wasn't 100, he didn't make it, and the book didn't sell. Case closed!

That having been said, the one thing I have learned in my 90 years now on this earth is that health has to do with exercising one's body and one's mind and having an ample supply of good luck.

W9-CBI-789